UNDERSTANDING LAMENTATIONS - REVISED

A commentary using Ancient Bible Study Methods

Michael Harvey Koplitz

Acknowledgment

This work could not have been accomplished without Dr. Anne Davis, who taught me Ancient (Hebraic) Bible study methods, and my two study partners, Rev. Dr. Robert Cook and Pastor Sandra Koplitz. We know that the journey has just started and will last a lifetime. The discovery of the depths of God's Word is waiting for us to find.

Michael Harvey Koplitz

Table of Contents

Introduction 7

   The main differences between the Greek method and the Hebraic method of teaching 9

Methodology 13

Chapter One 19

Process of Discovery 23

Chapter Two 39

Chapter Three 53

Language 53

Chapter Four 67

Chapter Five 77

Bibliography 83

Introduction

While I was attending Seminary earning my M. Div. degree, I started to question what the instructors and reference books were saying about the Scriptures. One of the ideas being offered then was that the Bible was full of errors and not factual. I found that attitude disturbing for Seminary instructors to be teaching. After all, the Seminary experience is to train pastors to go out into God's world and preach the Bible. How can you preach the Bible if you believe what these instructors are teaching? The methods that were being taught to examine the Bible just seemed inaccurate to me.

After graduating from Seminary, I spent much time reading different views about the Bible. I eventually read the Zohar. This collection of Midrashim is considered the secret work of the Torah, according to Kabbalists. Also, I learned quite a bit about Messianic Judaism. Their view of the Bible is quite different from the Seminary view.

I decided that the biblical interpretation that was being taught in Seminary was not the biblical interpretation the people heard when Jesus Christ (whose Hebraic name is Yeshua) preached. I went on a quest to learn what the people of Yeshua's day thought about Scripture, and what they thought when the Scriptures were read. This quest led me to Dr. Anne Davis and The Bible Learning University. Dr. Davis was in search of the same thing I was searching for. She had made many discoveries that helped me in my quest. I earned the Ph. D. degree from The Bible Learning University in Hebraic Studies in Christianity concentrating on ancient Bible Studies methods.

Finally, I found someone who believed that the church had placed almost 1900 years of theological ideas about the Scriptures and in many places possibly distorting its original meaning. What is also essential to hear is that the basic tenants of Yeshua as

God's Messiah, my Lord, and Savior are in the Bible. My faith in Yeshua is stronger now that I have learned from Dr. Davis how to study the Scriptures in the same manner that the people did in Yeshua's day.

I have included an article that describes the differences between Greek learning methods and Hebraic learning methods. Please do not skip this chapter unless you are familiar with ancient Bible study methods because if you do, then the analysis and commentary that follows may become difficult for you to understand.

Our God is vast and infinite, and so is His Word. May God bless you in your discovery of what God's Word is about.

The style of this book is different from the book of Jeremiah. The author of the book of Jeremiah was believed to be Baruch. This book was written by Jeremiah himself. It was the custom of Jeremiah's day to hire a professional writer. Jeremiah was an eyewitness to the destruction of the city of Jerusalem and the Temple by the Babylonian army. He weeps over the city and the Temple.

The original name of this book is *ekhah,* which means "alas." The Talmud refers to this book as Lamentations.[1]

---

[1] Rocco A. Errico and George M. Lamsa, *Aramaic Light on Ezra through the Song of Solomon* (Smyma, GA: Noohra Foundation, 2010).

The main differences between the Greek method and the Hebraic method of teaching

Once a student becomes aware of these two teaching styles, the student will be able to determine if the class attended or if a book read, whether the teaching method is either a Greek or Hebraic method. In the Greek manner, the instructor is always right because of advanced knowledge. In the college situation, it is because the professor has his/her Ph.D. in some area of study, so one assumes that he or she knows everything about the topic. For example, Rodney Dangerfield played the role of a middle-aged man going to college. His English midterm was to write about Kurt Vonnegut Jr. Since he did not understand any of Vonnegut's books he hired Vonnegut himself to write the midterm. When he received the paper from the English Professor told Dangerfield that whoever wrote the paper knew nothing about Vonnegut. The professor's words are an example of the Greek method of teaching. Did the Ph.D. English professor think that she knew more about Vonnegut's writings than Vonnegut did? [2]

In the Greek teaching method, the professor or the instructor claims to be the authority. If one attends a Bible study class and the class leader says, "I will teach you the only way to understand this biblical book," you may want to consider the implications. This method is standard since most Seminaries and Bible colleges teach a Greek mode of learning, which is the same method the church has been utilizing for centuries.

---

[2] *Back to School*. Performed by Rodney Dangerfield. Hollywood: CA: Paper Clip Productions, 1986. DVD.

Hebraic teaching methods are different. The teacher wants the students to challenge what they hear. It is through questioning that a student can learn. Also, the teacher wants his/her students to excel to a point where the student becomes the teacher.

If two rabbis come together to discuss a passage of Scripture, the result will be at least ten different opinions. All points of view are acceptable if each is supported by biblical evidence. It is permissible and encouraged that students develop many ideas. There is a depth to God's Word, and God wants us to find all His messages contained in the Scripture.

Seeking out the meaning of the Scriptures beyond the literal meaning is essential to understand God's Word fully.[3] The Greek method of learning the Scriptures has prevailed over the centuries. One problem is that only the literal interpretation of Scripture was often viewed as valid, as prompted by Martin Luther's "sola literalis" meaning that just the literal translation of Scripture was accurate. The Fundamentalist movements of today base their beliefs on the literal interpretation of the Scripture. Therefore, they do not believe that God placed more profound, hidden, or secret meanings in the Word.

The students of the Scriptures who learn through Hebraic training and understanding have drawn a different conclusion. The Hebrew language itself leads to different possible interpretations because of the construction of the language. The Hebraic method of Bible study opens avenues of thought about God's revelations in the Scripture never considered. Not all questions about the Scripture studied will have an

---

[3] Davis, Anne Kimball. *The Synoptic Gospels*. MP3. Albuquerque: NM: BibleInteract, 2012.

immediate answer. If so, it becomes the responsibility of the learners to uncover the meaning. Also, remember that many opinions about the meaning of Scripture are also acceptable.

Michael Harvey Koplitz

Methodology

The methodology employed is to use First Century Scripture study methods integrated with the customs and culture of Yeshua's day to examine the Hebrew and Christian Scriptures, thus gathering a more in-depth understanding by learning the Scriptures in the way the people of Yeshua's day did.

I have titled the methodology of analyzing a passage of Scripture in a Hebraic manner the "Process of Discovery." The author developed this methodology which brings together the various areas of linguistic and cultural understanding. There are several sections to the process, and not all the parts apply to every passage of Scripture. The overall result of developing this process is to give the reader a framework for studying the word in more depth.

The "Process of Discovery" starts with a Scripture passage. An examination of the linguistic structure of the passage is next. The linguistic structure includes parallelism, chiastic structures, and repetition. Formatting the passage in its linguistic form allows the reader to be able to visualize what the first century CE listener was hearing. Their corresponding sections label the chiasms, for example, A, B, C, B', A.' Not all passages of the Scriptures have a poetic form.

The next step is to "question the narrative." The questioning the narrative process assuming the reader knows nothing about the passage. Therefore, the questions go from the simple to the complex. The next task is to identify any linguistic patterns. Linguistic patterns include, but are not limited to irony, simile, metaphor, symbolism, idioms, hyperbole, figurative language, personification, and allegory.

A review of any translation inconsistencies discovered between the English NAU version and either the Hebrew or Greek versions is done. There are times when a Hebrew or Greek word is translated in more than one way. Inconsistencies also can be created by the translation committee, which may have decided to use traditional language instead of the actual translation. The decision of the translation committee is in the Preface or Introduction to the Bible. Perhaps some of the inconsistencies were intentionally added to convey some deeper meaning. An examination for every discrepancy is done.

The passage is analyzed for any echoes of the Hebrew Scriptures in the Christian Scriptures. Using a passage from the Hebrew Scriptures in the Christian Scriptures, an echo occurs.[4] Also, echoes are found when Torah (Genesis through Deuteronomy) passages , in other Hebrew Bible books. Cross-references in the Scripture are references from one verse to another verse which can assist the reader in understanding the verse.

The names of persons mentioned in the passage are listed. Many of the Hebrew names have meaning and may be associated with places or actions. Jewish parents used to name their children based on what they felt God had in store for their child. An example of this is Abraham whose original name was Abram and was changed to mean eternal father (God changed Abram's name to Abraham indicating a function he was to perform). When the Hebrew Bible gives names, many of the occurrences mean

---

[4] Mitzvot are the 613 commandments found in the Torah that please God. There are positive and negative commandments. The list was first development by Maimonides. The full list can be found at: ttp://www.jewfaq.org/613.htm.

something unique. The same importance can occur for the names of places. The time it takes to travel between locations can supply insight into the event.

Key phrases are identified in verses when they are essential to an understanding of that passage. There are no rules for selecting the keywords. Searching for other occurrences of the keywords in Scripture in a concordance is necessary to understand the word's usage; this must be done in either Hebrew or Greek, not in English. A classic Hebraic approach is to find the usage of a word in the Scripture by finding other verses that contain the word. The usage of a word, in its original language, is discovered by searching the Scripture in the language of the word. Verses that contain the word are identified, and a pattern for the usage of the word discovered. Each verse is examined to see what the usage of the word is which, may reveal a model for the word's usage. For Hebrew words the first usage of the word in the Scripture, primarily if used in the Torah, is essential. For the Greek words, the Christian Scriptures are used to determine the word usage in the Scripture. Sometimes finding the equivalent Greek word in the Septuagint then analyzing its usage in Hebrew can be very helpful.

The Rules of Hillel are used when applicable. Hillel was a Torah scholar who lived shortly before Yeshua's day. Hillel developed several rules for Torah students to interpret the Scriptures which refer to halachic Midrash. In several cases, these rules are helpful in the analysis of the Scripture.

The cultural implications from the period of the writing are done after the linguistic analysis is completed. The culture is crucial because it is not explicitly referenced in the biblical narratives as indicated earlier.

From the linguistic analysis and the cultural understanding, it is possible to obtain a deeper meaning of the Scripture beyond the literal meaning of the plain text. That is what the listeners of Yeshua's time were doing. They put the linguistics and culture together without even having to contemplate it. They simply did it.

The analysis will lead to a set of findings explaining what the passage meant in Yeshua's day. Most of the time, the Hebraic analysis leads to the desire for more in-depth analysis to fully understand what Yeshua was talking about or what was happening to Him. Whatever the result, a new, more in-depth understanding of the Scripture is obtained.

The components of the Process of Discovery are:

Language

   Process of Discovery

     Linguistics Section

       Linguistic Structure

       Discussion

       Questioning the Passage

       Verse Comparison of citations or proof text

       Translation Inconsistencies

       Biblical Personalities

       Biblical Locations

       Phrase Study

       Scripture cross-references

       Linguistic Echoes

       Rules of Hillel

Culture Section

   Discussion

Questioning the passage

Cultural Echoes

Culture and Linguistics Section

Discussion

Thoughts

Reflections

Only the areas needed for each chapter is included.

Chapter One

New American Standard 1995	Hebrew

New American Standard 1995

1 How lonely sits the city That was full of people! She has become like a widow Who was *once* great among the nations! She who was a princess among the provinces Has become a forced laborer!

2 She weeps bitterly in the night And her tears are on her cheeks; She has none to comfort her Among all her lovers. All her friends have dealt treacherously with her; They have become her enemies.

3 Judah has gone into exile under affliction And under harsh servitude; She dwells among the nations, *But* she has found no rest; All her pursuers have overtaken her In the midst of distress.

4 The roads of Zion are in mourning Because no one comes to the appointed feasts. All her gates are desolate; Her priests are groaning, Her virgins are afflicted, And she herself is bitter.

5 Her adversaries have become her masters, Her enemies prosper; For the LORD has caused her grief Because of the multitude of her transgressions; Her little ones have gone away As captives before the adversary.

6 All her majesty Has departed from the daughter of Zion; Her princes have become like deer That have found no pasture; And they have fled without strength Before the pursuer.

7 In the days of her affliction and homelessness Jerusalem remembers all her precious things That were from the

Hebrew

א אֵיכָה ׀ יָשְׁבָה בָדָד הָעִיר רַבָּתִי עָם הָיְתָה כְּאַלְמָנָה רַבָּתִי בַגּוֹיִם שָׂרָתִי בַּמְּדִינוֹת הָיְתָה לָמַס׃ ס

ב בָּכוֹ תִבְכֶּה בַּלַּיְלָה וְדִמְעָתָהּ עַל לֶחֱיָהּ אֵין־לָהּ מְנַחֵם מִכָּל־אֹהֲבֶיהָ כָּל־רֵעֶיהָ בָּגְדוּ בָהּ הָיוּ לָהּ לְאֹיְבִים׃ ס

ג גָּלְתָה יְהוּדָה מֵעֹנִי וּמֵרֹב עֲבֹדָה הִיא יָשְׁבָה בַגּוֹיִם לֹא מָצְאָה מָנוֹחַ כָּל־רֹדְפֶיהָ הִשִּׂיגוּהָ בֵּין הַמְּצָרִים׃ ס

ד דַּרְכֵי צִיּוֹן אֲבֵלוֹת מִבְּלִי בָּאֵי מוֹעֵד כָּל־שְׁעָרֶיהָ שׁוֹמֵמִין כֹּהֲנֶיהָ נֶאֱנָחִים בְּתוּלֹתֶיהָ נּוּגוֹת וְהִיא מַר־לָהּ׃ ס

ה הָיוּ צָרֶיהָ לְרֹאשׁ אֹיְבֶיהָ שָׁלוּ כִּי־יְהוָה הוֹגָהּ עַל רֹב־פְּשָׁעֶיהָ עוֹלָלֶיהָ הָלְכוּ שְׁבִי לִפְנֵי־צָר׃ ס

ו וַיֵּצֵא (מִן־בַּת־)[מִבַּת־]צִיּוֹן כָּל־הֲדָרָהּ הָיוּ שָׂרֶיהָ כְּאַיָּלִים לֹא־מָצְאוּ מִרְעֶה וַיֵּלְכוּ בְלֹא־כֹחַ לִפְנֵי רוֹדֵף׃ ס

ז זָכְרָה יְרוּשָׁלַםִ יְמֵי עָנְיָהּ וּמְרוּדֶיהָ כֹּל מַחֲמֻדֶיהָ אֲשֶׁר הָיוּ מִימֵי קֶדֶם בִּנְפֹל עַמָּהּ בְּיַד־צָר וְאֵין עוֹזֵר לָהּ רָאוּהָ צָרִים שָׂחֲקוּ עַל מִשְׁבַּתֶּהָ׃ ס

ח חֵטְא חָטְאָה יְרוּשָׁלַםִ עַל־כֵּן לְנִידָה הָיָתָה כָּל־מְכַבְּדֶיהָ הִזִּילוּהָ כִּי־רָאוּ עֶרְוָתָהּ גַּם־הִיא נֶאֶנְחָה וַתָּשָׁב אָחוֹר׃ ס

ט טֻמְאָתָהּ בְּשׁוּלֶיהָ לֹא זָכְרָה אַחֲרִיתָהּ וַתֵּרֶד פְּלָאִים אֵין מְנַחֵם לָהּ רְאֵה יְהוָה אֶת־עָנְיִי כִּי הִגְדִּיל אוֹיֵב׃ ס

days of old, When her people fell into the hand of the adversary And no one helped her. The adversaries saw her, They mocked at her ruin.

⁸ Jerusalem sinned greatly, Therefore she has become an unclean thing. All who honored her despise her Because they have seen her nakedness; Even she herself groans and turns away.

⁹ Her uncleanness was in her skirts; She did not consider her future. Therefore she has fallen astonishingly; She has no comforter. "See, O LORD, my affliction, For the enemy has magnified himself!"

¹⁰ The adversary has stretched out his hand Over all her precious things, For she has seen the nations enter her sanctuary, The ones whom You commanded That they should not enter into Your congregation.

¹¹ All her people groan seeking bread; They have given their precious things for food To restore their lives themselves. "See, O LORD, and look, For I am despised."

¹² "Is it nothing to all you who pass this way? Look and see if there is any pain like my pain Which was severely dealt out to me, Which the LORD inflicted on the day of His fierce anger.

¹³ "From on high He sent fire into my bones, And it prevailed *over them*. He has spread a net for my feet; He has turned me back; He has made me desolate, Faint all day long.

¹⁴ "The yoke of my transgressions is bound; By His hand they are knit together. They have come upon my neck; He has made my strength fail. The Lord has given me into the hands Of *those against whom* I am not able to stand.

יָדוֹ פָּרַשׂ צָר עַל כָּל־מַחֲמַדֶּיהָ כִּי־ ¹⁰
רָאֲתָה גוֹיִם בָּאוּ מִקְדָּשָׁהּ אֲשֶׁר צִוִּיתָה
לֹא־יָבֹאוּ בַקָּהָל לָךְ׃ ס

כָּל־עַמָּהּ נֶאֱנָחִים מְבַקְשִׁים לֶחֶם ¹¹
נָתְנוּ (מַחֲמוֹדֵּיהֶם) [מַחֲמַדֵּיהֶם] בְּאֹכֶל
לְהָשִׁיב נָפֶשׁ רְאֵה יְהוָה וְהַבִּיטָה כִּי
הָיִיתִי זוֹלֵלָה׃ ס

לוֹא אֲלֵיכֶם כָּל־עֹבְרֵי דֶרֶךְ הַבִּיטוּ ¹²
וּרְאוּ אִם־יֵשׁ מַכְאוֹב כְּמַכְאֹבִי אֲשֶׁר
עוֹלַל לִי אֲשֶׁר הוֹגָה יְהוָה בְּיוֹם חֲרוֹן
אַפּוֹ׃ ס

מִמָּרוֹם שָׁלַח־אֵשׁ בְּעַצְמֹתַי וַיִּרְדֶּנָּה ¹³
פָּרַשׂ רֶשֶׁת לְרַגְלַי הֱשִׁיבַנִי אָחוֹר נְתָנַנִי
שֹׁמֵמָה כָּל־הַיּוֹם דָּוָה׃ ס

נִשְׂקַד עֹל פְּשָׁעַי בְּיָדוֹ יִשְׂתָּרְגוּ עָלוּ ¹⁴
עַל־צַוָּארִי הִכְשִׁיל כֹּחִי נְתָנַנִי אֲדֹנָי בִּידֵי
לֹא־אוּכַל קוּם׃ ס

סִלָּה כָל־אַבִּירַי אֲדֹנָי בְּקִרְבִּי קָרָא ¹⁵
עָלַי מוֹעֵד לִשְׁבֹּר בַּחוּרָי גַּת דָּרַךְ אֲדֹנָי
לִבְתוּלַת בַּת־יְהוּדָה׃ ס

עַל־אֵלֶּה אֲנִי בוֹכִיָּה עֵינִי עֵינִי יֹרְדָה ¹⁶
מַּיִם כִּי־רָחַק מִמֶּנִּי מְנַחֵם מֵשִׁיב נַפְשִׁי
הָיוּ בָנַי שׁוֹמֵמִים כִּי גָבַר אוֹיֵב׃ ס

פֵּרְשָׂה צִיּוֹן בְּיָדֶיהָ אֵין מְנַחֵם לָהּ צִוָּה ¹⁷
יְהוָה לְיַעֲקֹב סְבִיבָיו צָרָיו הָיְתָה
יְרוּשָׁלַם לְנִדָּה בֵּינֵיהֶם׃ ס

צַדִּיק הוּא יְהוָה כִּי פִיהוּ מָרִיתִי ¹⁸
שִׁמְעוּ־נָא כָל־(עַמִּים) [הָעַמִּים] וּרְאוּ
מַכְאֹבִי בְּתוּלֹתַי וּבַחוּרַי הָלְכוּ בַשֶּׁבִי׃ ס

קָרָאתִי לַמְאַהֲבַי הֵמָּה רִמּוּנִי כֹּהֲנַי ¹⁹
וּזְקֵנַי בָּעִיר גָּוָעוּ כִּי־בִקְשׁוּ אֹכֶל לָמוֹ
וְיָשִׁיבוּ אֶת־נַפְשָׁם׃ ס

15 "The Lord has rejected all my strong men In my midst; He has called an appointed time against me To crush my young men; The Lord has trodden *as in* a wine press The virgin daughter of Judah.

16 "For these things I weep; My eyes run down with water; Because far from me is a comforter, One who restores my soul. My children are desolate Because the enemy has prevailed."

17 Zion stretches out her hands; There is no one to comfort her; The LORD has commanded concerning Jacob That the ones round about him should be his adversaries; Jerusalem has become an unclean thing among them.

18 "The LORD is righteous; For I have rebelled against His command; Hear now, all peoples, And behold my pain; My virgins and my young men Have gone into captivity.

19 "I called to my lovers, *but* they deceived me; My priests and my elders perished in the city While they sought food to restore their strength themselves.

20 "See, O LORD, for I am in distress; My spirit is greatly troubled; My heart is overturned within me, For I have been very rebellious. In the street the sword slays; In the house it is like death.

21 "They have heard that I groan; There is no one to comfort me; All my enemies have heard of my calamity; They are glad that You have done *it*. Oh, that You would bring the day which You have proclaimed, That they may become like me.

22 "Let all their wickedness come before You; And deal with them as You have dealt with me For all my transgressions;

רְאֵ֨ה יְהוָ֤ה כִּֽי־צַר־לִ�֙ מֵעַ֣י חֳמַרְמָ֔רוּ נֶהְפַּ֤ךְ לִבִּי֙ בְּקִרְבִּ֔י כִּ֥י מָר֖וֹ מָרִ֑יתִי מִח֥וּץ שִׁכְּלָה־חֶ֖רֶב בַּבַּ֥יִת כַּמָּֽוֶת׃ ס 20

שָׁמְע֗וּ כִּ֤י נֶאֱנָחָה֙ אָ֔נִי אֵ֥ין מְנַחֵ֖ם לִ֑י כָּל־אֹ֨יְבַ֜י שָׁמְע֤וּ רָֽעָתִי֙ שָׂ֔שׂוּ כִּ֥י אַתָּ֖ה עָשִׂ֑יתָ הֵבֵ֛אתָ יוֹם־קָרָ֖אתָ וְיִֽהְי֥וּ כָמֽוֹנִי׃ ס 21

תָּבֹ֨א כָל־רָעָתָ֤ם לְפָנֶ֙יךָ֙ וְעוֹלֵ֣ל לָ֔מוֹ כַּאֲשֶׁ֥ר עוֹלַ֖לְתָּ לִ֑י עַ֖ל כָּל־פְּשָׁעָ֑י כִּֽי־רַבּ֥וֹת אַנְחֹתַ֖י וְלִבִּ֥י דַוָּֽי׃ פ 22

For my groans are many and my heart is faint."	

For my groans are many and my heart is
faint."

Process of Discovery

Linguistics Section

Linguistic Structure

A [1] How lonely sits the city That was full of people! She has become like a widow Who was *once* great among the nations! She who was a princess among the provinces Has become a forced laborer!

B [2] She weeps bitterly in the night And her tears are on her cheeks; She has none to comfort her Among all her lovers. All her friends have dealt treacherously with her; They have become her enemies.

C [3] Judah has gone into exile under affliction And under harsh servitude; She dwells among the nations, *But* she has found no rest; All her pursuers have overtaken her In the midst of distress.

D [4] The roads of Zion are in mourning Because no one comes to the appointed feasts. All her gates are desolate; Her priests are groaning, Her virgins are afflicted, And she herself is bitter.

E [5] Her adversaries have become her masters, Her enemies prosper; For the LORD has caused her grief Because of the multitude of her transgressions; Her little ones have gone away As captives before the adversary.

F [6] All her majesty Has departed from the daughter of Zion; Her princes have become like deer That have found no pasture; And they have fled without strength Before the pursuer.

G [7] In the days of her affliction and homelessness Jerusalem remembers all her precious things That were from the days of old, When her people fell into the hand of the adversary And no one helped her. The adversaries saw her, They mocked at her ruin.

H [8] Jerusalem sinned greatly, Therefore she has become an unclean thing. All who honored her despise her Because they have seen her nakedness; Even she herself groans and turns away.

I [9] Her uncleanness was in her skirts; She did not consider her future. Therefore she has fallen astonishingly; She has no comforter. "See, O LORD, my affliction, For the enemy has magnified himself!"

J [10] The adversary has stretched out his hand Over all her precious things, For she has seen the nations enter her sanctuary, The ones whom You commanded That they should not enter into Your congregation.

K [11] All her people groan seeking bread; They have given their precious things for food To restore their lives themselves. "See, O LORD, and look, For I am despised."

K' [12] "Is it nothing to all you who pass this way? Look and see if there is any pain like my pain Which was severely dealt out to me, Which the LORD inflicted on the day of His fierce anger.

J' [13] "From on high He sent fire into my bones, And it prevailed *over them*. He has spread a net for my feet; He has turned me back; He has made me desolate, Faint all day long.

I' [14] "The yoke of my transgressions is bound; By His hand they are knit together. They have come upon my neck; He has made my strength fail. The Lord has given me into the hands Of *those against whom* I am not able to stand.

H' [15] "The Lord has rejected all my strong men In my midst; He has called an appointed time against me To crush my young men; The Lord has trodden *as in* a wine press The virgin daughter of Judah.

G' [16] "For these things I weep; My eyes run down with water; Because far from me is a comforter, One who restores my soul. My children are desolate Because the enemy has prevailed."

F' [17] Zion stretches out her hands; There is no one to comfort her; The LORD has commanded concerning Jacob That the ones round about him should be his adversaries; Jerusalem has become an unclean thing among them.

E' [18] "The LORD is righteous; For I have rebelled against His command; Hear now, all peoples, And behold my pain; My virgins and my young men Have gone into captivity.

D' [19] "I called to my lovers, *but* they deceived me; My priests and my elders perished in the city While they sought food to restore their strength themselves.

C' [20] "See, O LORD, for I am in distress; My spirit is greatly troubled; My heart is overturned within me, For I have been very rebellious. In the street the sword slays; In the house it is like death.

B' [21] "They have heard that I groan; There is no one to comfort me; All my enemies have heard of my calamity; They are glad that You have done *it*. Oh, that You would bring the day which You have proclaimed, That they may become like me.

A' [22] "Let all their wickedness come before You; And deal with them as You have dealt with me For all my transgressions; For my groans are many and my heart is faint."

A: Lamentation. B: No one to console. C: Sufferings. D: Priests. E: Rebellion. F: No one to console. G: No one to console. H: Her sufferings. I: Dirty. J: Devastation. K: To see.[5]

Discussion

The lamentations are about the destruction of Jerusalem and the Temple of the LORD. The once-strong nation of Israel was reduced to becoming slaves. To fully understand the book of Lamentations, it is crucial to examine the history of Judea at that time.

---

[5] Hajime Murai, "Literary Structure (Chiasm, Chiasmus) of Book of Lamentations," Literary structure (chiasm, chiasmus) of each pericopes of Book of Lamentations, accessed April 21, 2020, http://www.bible.literarystructure.info/bible/25_Lamentations_pericope_e.html.

A chronology of the First Temple

3316 – Yehoyakim bim Yoshiahu becomes King of Judah

[36] Jehoiakim was twenty-five years old when he became king, and he reigned eleven years in Jerusalem; and his mother's name *was* Zebidah the daughter of Pedaiah of Rumah. [37] He did evil in the sight of the LORD, according to all that his fathers had done. (2 Ki. 23:36-37 NAU)

3320 – Nebuchadnezzar, king of Babylon, conquered Judea. He removed part of the Temple's holy vessels and took the royal family's children to Babylon.

In the third year of the reign of Jehoiakim king of Judah, Nebuchadnezzar king of Babylon came to Jerusalem and besieged it. (Dan. 1:1 NAU)

3327 – Yehoyachim ben Yehoyakim became king and reigned for only three months. Nebuchadnezzar exiled him to Babylon together with 10,000 people and the Torah sages.

[16] All the men of valor, seven thousand, and the craftsmen and the smiths, one thousand, all strong and fit for war, and these the king of Babylon brought into exile to Babylon. (2 Ki. 24:16 NAU)

3327 – Zedekiah ben Yehoyakim becomes the last King of Judea

[18] Zedekiah was twenty-one years old when he became king, and he reigned eleven years in Jerusalem; and his mother's name was Hamutal the daughter of Jeremiah of Libnah. (2 Ki. 24:18 NAU)

3338 - the first Temple was destroyed. It had stood for 410 years

Questioning the narrative[6]

1. What city is being referred to in verse one?

    The book of Lamentations is about the siege Nebuchadnezzar brought to Jerusalem. Therefore, the city referred to in this verse is Jerusalem.

1. What is the symbolism of a widow in verse one?

    The widow symbolizes the city of Jerusalem. When the people were exiled, the city became void of inhabitants. The widow was awaiting the return of her husband. The Talmud stresses the prefix כ because the city would only be a widow for a brief time. The symbolism also relates to a woman whose husband has left for a foreign land but intends to return. Therefore, she is only widowed for a small amount of time.

    Another viewpoint is that the city of Jerusalem was widowed because all of the tribes of Israel were gone. Nevertheless, the town knew that God would never desert her.[7]

2. What is the symbolism of being a forced laborer in verse one?

    The Hebrew word מַס can be translated as "forced laborer" or as a "tributary." Refer to the word study section.

---

[6] (The answers offered are for discussion purposes. You may have different answers. Remember all answers must be defendable from Scripture. This applies to this section and to the Culture Section.)

[7] Zlotowitz, Meir, and Nosson Scherman. "Chapter 1." *Megillas Eichah = Lamentations: A New Translation with a Commentary Anthologized from Talmudic, Midrashic and Rabbinic Sources*. New York: Mesorah Publications, 1979. N. pag. Print.

A historical definition of the tributary is a person or state that pays tribute to another state or ruler. [8]

2. What does it mean that the city weeps at night? (v. 2)

   This verse starts with the word "weeping," and the second word of the sentence is also translated as weeping. Therefore, we have what the sages call double weeping. What is interesting is that the second weeping is in the future tense. Therefore, the lamentation is to cry bitterly for Jerusalem in the present, when the Babylonian army was invading, and for some future event. The sages say that the future event was the destruction of the second Temple in Jerusalem. [9]

3. Who were her lovers? (v. 2)

   This is an irony, which is found in the Hebrew Scriptures, that the enemies of Jerusalem were called her lovers. Obviously, since the enemies of Jerusalem did invade and conquer her, under the direction and in conjunction with the Babylonian army, calling them lovers shows the irony. [10]

4. What were the affliction and harsh servitude? (v. 3)

   Judah worshiped false gods, thus committing idolatry. When they were taken into Babylon, their affliction and harsh servitude were that they were forced to serve the false gods of Babylon.

---

[8] "Tributary." *Wikipedia*. Wikimedia Foundation, n.d. Web. 28 Sept. 2016. Accessed April 20, 2020.
[9] Zlotowitz, Meir, and Nosson Scherman. "Chapter 1." *Megillas Eichah = Lamentations: A New Translation with a Commentary Anthologized from Talmudic, Midrashic and Rabbinic Sources*. New York: Mesorah Publications, 1979. N. pag. Print.
[10] IBID

5. What are the appointed feasts? (v. 4)

> The appointed feasts are Passover, unleavened bread, first fruits of the harvest, Shavuot, Rosh Hashanah, Yom Kippur, and Sukkoth.[11]

3. In verse four, what is the symbolism of "the roads of Zion are in mourning"?

> The roads of Zion were the roads that led to Jerusalem. The roads we in mourning because there were no Jews on the roads because they had been taken into exile.

6. Who were Judah's adversaries? (v. 5)

> Judah's enemies at that time were just about all its surrounding nations and the Babylonians. When the Babylonian army made its way south, the lands' peoples knew they were coming after Judah. Therefore, they aligned themselves with Babylon as a means of survival.

7. What were Judah's transgressions? (v. 5)

> Judah's transgressions were the adoption of the cult worship practiced by the Canaan peoples who lived in the land before them.

8. What was Judah's majesty? (v. 6)

> Judah's majesty was that the LORD was with Judah, residing in the Temple. The spirit of the LORD departed the Temple before it was destroyed. Besides, the Sanhedrin, the sages, and the priests were taken away from Judah during the exile. The Temple and these people listed were the majesties of Judah.

---

[11] "THE SEVEN ANNUAL SACRED FEASTS OF THE OLD COVENANT: The Feasts of Remembrance." THE SEVEN ANNUAL SACRED FEASTS OF THE OLD COVENANT: The Feasts of Remembrance. Accessed May 1, 2020. http://www.agapebiblestudy.com/charts/Seven%20Sacred%20Feasts%20of%20the%20Old%20Covenant.htm.

9. What does the simile "princes like deer" mean? (v. 6)

   The princes were the leaders of Jerusalem, and they did not rebuke one another, nor the people when they saw the transgressions against the LORD that the people were doing. During intense heat, deer turn their face toward one another. Thus, they cannot see what other deer are doing. This simile says that the leadership of Jerusalem was not concerned about what was happening with the people and turned a blind eye.[12]

10. Who were the pursuers? (v. 6)

    The pursuers were the allies of the Babylonian army. They captured the people fleeing from the Babylonians through the southern border of Judea. These were mainly the Edomites.

11. What does "her uncleanliness was in her skirts" mean? (v. 9)

    The Targum reads, "The uncleanliness of her menstrual blood was in her skirts." Menstrual blood is symbolic of the sins of the people. "It was in her skirts" is symbolic of trying to hide. The people of Jerusalem were hiding their sins. Their sins were that they worshiped idols.

    The sage Rashi[i] said that this meant that the sins of the people were obvious and out in the open. The sage Alshich[ii] said this phrase was an allusion to the time of Destruction when the sinners hid their sins behind locked doors, worshiping idols.[13]

---

[12] IBID

[13] Zlotowitz, Meir, and Nosson Scherman. "Chapter 1." *Megillas Eichah = Lamentations: A New Translation with a Commentary Anthologized from Talmudic, Midrashic and Rabbinic Sources*. New York: Mesorah Publications, 1979. N. pag. Print.

12. Who were the nations that the LORD ordered not to enter the Temple? (v. 10)

The LORD ordered that Moabites and Ammonites were never to enter the Temple. The military took gold and silver objects when the armies broke into the Temple. The Moabites and Ammonites went to grab the Torah, so they could expunge the LORD's order for them not to enter the Temple.

Deut. 23:3 "No Ammonite or Moabite shall enter the assembly of the LORD; none of their *descendants,* even to the tenth generation, shall ever enter the assembly of the LORD

13. What is verse eleven referring to?

During the Babylonian siege of Jerusalem, the people starved. Bread became scarce, forcing people to trade their valuables for food. The book Tiferes Uziel written by Rabbi Hagaon Uziel Meislish (born in 1743, died in 1785), says that the people were so concerned about their existence they became oblivious to the tragedy that was to befall the nation.[14]

14. What is the day of the LORD's fierce anger? (v. 12)

The day of the LORD's fierce anger is the ninth day of Av. On this day, several calamities came to the Jewish people.[15]

15. What does it mean to have fire in my bones? (v. 13)

Jeremiah is referring to the destruction of the Temple and the city. The fire was used by the invading army to destroy the Temple. The net referred to in verse thireen refers to the army that surrounded the city so that no one escaped.

---

[14] IBID.
[15] IBID.

Jeremiah felt that the LORD had turned His back on the people. Since the people turned their backs to the LORD by worshiping idols, the LORD did the same. To many readers of the Hebrew Scriptures, they get the impression that the LORD is a vengeful God. That is not the truth of the Scriptures. In this verse, Jeremiah explains that the LORD turned away from Israel because Israel broke the covenant with the LORD to the point that something had to happen. What happened was that the LORD removed His protection from Israel. This change allowed the nations of the world to invade and capture Israel. It was the people's fault. They made a covenant with the LORD at Mount Sinai to obey the Torah. They had not been following the Torah. The protection promised at Sinai included faithfulness. When faithfulness left Israel, so did the LORD's protection.

16. What does it mean that the LORD knitted the transgressions of the people? (v. 14)

It was believed that the LORD did not punish Israel for each of her transgressions. Instead, the LORD grouped them into one significant transgression, thus knitting them together. The huge transgression was placed upon the people; therefore, they could not fight the siege. The LORD gave the people into the hands of the Babylonians meant that the invaders won the war.

17. What does it mean that the virgin daughter of Israel was trodden as in a winepress? (v. 15)

The Targum says that the invaders defiled the virgins of the city. So many virgins were defiled that the collected blood of their virginity was as large as wine coming out of a winepress when a man treads on the grapes. Raping women, especially virgins, was a sign of taking revenge on conquered people for the soldiers they lost during the battle. Virgins spill blood when they have sexual intercourse for the first time.[16]

18. What is verse seventeen referring to?

The Targum says that the LORD enjoined His Torah upon Israel (the House of Jacob). The people, over the years, had continually transgressed the Law and decrees of the LORD. Therefore, the oppressors of Israel surrounded the country and destroyed it. Jerusalem had become a city of sinners.[17]

19. Who were Israel's lovers? (v. 19)

At the time of the invasion, the leaders of Judah thought the surrounding nations were their friends. When the invasion occurred, the surrounding nations banded with Babylon. Perhaps the leaders of these nations realized that resistance was futile. Instead, they joined Babylon. When the invasion was over, the surrounding nations of Judah were allowed to plunder anything the Babylonians left behind. These nations were allowed to take anything off the land that they wished.

20. What does verse twenty-one say?

This verse is a curse on the surrounding nations that Judah thought were allies but attacked Babylon instead. Jeremiah asked the LORD to have the same thing happen to them as what happened to Judah. The curse continues into verse twenty-two.

---

[16] Martin McNamara, Kevin J. Cathcart, and Michael Maher, *The Aramaic Bible: the Targums* (Wilmington, DE: M. Glazier, 1987).
[17] IBID.

Phrase Study

1. **מַס** mas or **מִס** mis, Meaning: a body of forced laborers, forced service, task workers, taskwork, serfdom[18]

   > ^{NAU} Genesis 49:15 "When he saw that a resting place was good And that the land was pleasant, He bowed his shoulder to bear burdens, And became a slave at forced labor. (Gen. 49:15 NAU)

   > ^{NAU} Exodus 1:11 So they appointed taskmasters over them to afflict them with hard labor. And they built for Pharaoh storage cities, Pithom and Raamses. (Exod. 1:11 NAU)

   > ^{NAU} Deuteronomy 20:11 "If it agrees to make peace with you and opens to you, then all the people who are found in it shall become your forced labor and shall serve you.

   Conclusion: The primary usage of this word is "forced labor." In the Exodus passage listed above, instead of "forced labor," the translation of "afflict them with hard labor" is used. These two phrases mean the same thing. When the Babylonians took the Israelites into exile, they forced them to work for the Babylonians. The forced labor could also be considered the worship of the Babylonian god Marduk.

Culture Section

Discussion

The people thought the LORD had sent the Babylonians to destroy the city of Jerusalem and the Temple because of the people's sins. The abominations and

---

[18] Robert Laird. Harris, *Theological Word Book of the Old Testament*, 1981.

transgressions were completed when Baal worship was not only done in the Temple but also in the Sanctum Sanctorum.

Questioning the passage

1. What does "her virgins as afflicted" mean? (v. 4)

    When the Babylonian army invaded Jerusalem and Judah, they took the women of the land and the city and raped them. The word "afflicted" is better translated as "to humiliate" or "to ravish." Therefore, the Babylonian army defiled the women of Judah and Jerusalem. This was common in wartime because it expressed vengeance against the enemy's vanquished troops. The Babylonian military also had mercenaries from the Moabites, Ammonites, and Edomites. [19]

Culture and Linguistics Section

Discussion

The culture of the people in Judea had changed over the years from what it was at the time of King David and King Solomon to what it was when the Babylonian army invaded Jerusalem. There were ebbs and flows of time where Yahweh worship was the only type in the land. There were periods when Baal worship occurred. The lament over the loss of Jerusalem and the Temple is understandable by Jeremiah, who happened to be a prophet of the LORD. However, how could the Lord continue to let His Temple, his home on earth,

---

[19] Lamsa, George M., Rocco Errico A. "Lamentations" In *Aramaic Light on Isaiah, Jeremiah, and Lamentations*, by Smyrna: Noorah, 2011.

stand when the people were violating it and defiling it with their acts, words, and deeds. Unfortunately, Judea did not create alliances and friendships. Therefore, when the Babylonians came from the north, all they needed to do was make some small promises to the outlying countries. They might have rallied together to defeat their enemy, the Babylonians.

Additional information from the Targum

According to the Targum of Lamentations, the ninth day of Av on the Hebraic calendar is when Jerusalem's first and second Temple was destroyed. This day was also when the spies that Moses sent into the promised land came back and gave their report that the people of the land were giants and that Israel could not conquer the land. In addition, World War I started on this day, and Hebraic scholars believe that the war did not stop until the end of World War II. On each of these events, a radical tragedy occurred with the death of many Jews.

The Targum equates the exile to Babylon to that of Adam and Eve. They were exiled from the garden of Eden because of sin.

Thoughts

Jeremiah was an eyewitness to the tragedy of the Temple of the LORD being destroyed. Besides, he witnessed the destruction of the city and Jerusalem. He saw the invaders rape women and kill men and children. From Jeremiah's point of view, the LORD sent His punishment upon the city. The city was not following the Laws of the LORD that they agreed to at Sinai. Jeremiah believed that the invasion was because of the sins of the people. As noted earlier, the LORD did not have to punish

Judah. He took away His protection. The Ten Commandments is a treaty between the LORD and Israel. The LORD said He would protect His people if they followed the Torah. The people agreed at Sinai but then, during the centuries, turned away from the LORD and to idol worship. The LORD gathered the people's transgressions, eventually committing them to a massive punishment. If the people had repented and turned to the LORD on the eighth day of Av, the LORD would have protected them. The LORD's protection happened when the Assyrians laid siege to Jerusalem. The people repented, and the LORD drove off the Assyrians. During the Babylonian siege, the people could have repented. They did not. The result was the destruction of the city, the Temple, and the people's Exile.

Michael Harvey Koplitz

New American Standard 1995	Hebrew

[1] How the Lord has covered the daughter of Zion With a cloud in His anger! He has cast from Heaven to earth The glory of Israel, And has not remembered His footstool In the day of His anger.

[2] The Lord has swallowed up; He has not spared All the habitations of Jacob. In His wrath He has thrown down The strongholds of the daughter of Judah; He has brought *them* down to the ground; He has profaned the kingdom and its princes.

[3] In fierce anger He has cut off All the strength of Israel; He has drawn back His right hand From before the enemy. And He has burned in Jacob like a flaming fire Consuming round about.

[4] He has bent His bow like an enemy; He has set His right hand like an adversary And slain all that were pleasant to the eye; In the tent of the daughter of Zion He has poured out His wrath like fire.

[5] The Lord has become like an enemy. He has swallowed up Israel; He has swallowed up all its palaces, He has destroyed its strongholds And multiplied in the daughter of Judah Mourning and moaning.

[6] And He has violently treated His tabernacle like a garden *booth*; He has destroyed His appointed meeting place. The LORD has caused to be forgotten The appointed feast and sabbath in Zion, And He has despised king and priest In the indignation of His anger.

אֵיכָה֩ יָעִ֨יב בְּאַפּ֤וֹ ׀ אֲדֹנָי֙ אֶת־בַּת־צִיּ֔וֹן הִשְׁלִ֤יךְ מִשָּׁמַ֙יִם֙ אֶ֔רֶץ תִּפְאֶ֖רֶת יִשְׂרָאֵ֑ל וְלֹא־זָכַ֥ר הֲדֹם־רַגְלָ֖יו בְּי֥וֹם אַפּֽוֹ׃ ס [2] בִּלַּ֨ע אֲדֹנָ֜י (לא) [וְלֹ֣א] חָמַ֗ל אֵ֚ת כָּל־נְא֣וֹת יַעֲקֹ֔ב הָרַ֧ס בְּעֶבְרָת֛וֹ מִבְצְרֵ֥י בַת־יְהוּדָ֖ה הִגִּ֣יעַ לָאָ֑רֶץ חִלֵּ֥ל מַמְלָכָ֖ה וְשָׂרֶֽיהָ׃ ס [3] גָּדַ֣ע בָּֽחֳרִי־אַ֗ף כֹּ֚ל קֶ֣רֶן יִשְׂרָאֵ֔ל הֵשִׁ֥יב אָח֛וֹר יְמִינ֖וֹ מִפְּנֵ֣י אוֹיֵ֑ב וַיִּבְעַ֤ר בְּיַעֲקֹב֙ כְּאֵ֣שׁ לֶֽהָבָ֔ה אָכְלָ֖ה סָבִֽיב׃ ס [4] דָּרַ֨ךְ קַשְׁתּ֜וֹ כְּאוֹיֵ֗ב נִצָּ֤ב יְמִינוֹ֙ כְּצָ֔ר וַֽיַּהֲרֹ֔ג כֹּ֖ל מַחֲמַדֵּי־עָ֑יִן בְּאֹ֙הֶל֙ בַּת־צִיּ֔וֹן שָׁפַ֥ךְ כָּאֵ֖שׁ חֲמָתֽוֹ׃ ס [5] הָיָ֨ה אֲדֹנָ֤י ׀ כְּאוֹיֵב֙ בִּלַּ֣ע יִשְׂרָאֵ֔ל בִּלַּע֙ כָּל־אַרְמְנוֹתֶ֔יהָ שִׁחֵ֖ת מִבְצָרָ֑יו וַיֶּ֙רֶב֙ בְּבַת־יְהוּדָ֔ה תַּאֲנִיָּ֖ה וַאֲנִיָּֽה׃ ס [6] וַיַּחְמֹ֤ס כַּגַּן֙ שֻׂכּ֔וֹ שִׁחֵ֖ת מוֹעֲד֑וֹ שִׁכַּ֨ח יְהוָ֤ה ׀ בְּצִיּוֹן֙ מוֹעֵ֣ד וְשַׁבָּ֔ת וַיִּנְאַ֥ץ בְּזַֽעַם־אַפּ֖וֹ מֶ֥לֶךְ וְכֹהֵֽן׃ ס [7] זָנַ֨ח אֲדֹנָ֤י ׀ מִזְבְּחוֹ֙ נִאֵ֣ר מִקְדָּשׁ֔וֹ הִסְגִּ֛יר בְּיַד־אוֹיֵ֖ב חוֹמֹ֣ת אַרְמְנוֹתֶ֑יהָ ק֛וֹל נָתְנ֥וּ בְּבֵית־יְהוָ֖ה כְּי֥וֹם מוֹעֵֽד׃ ס [8] חָשַׁ֨ב יְהוָ֤ה ׀ לְהַשְׁחִית֙ חוֹמַ֣ת בַּת־צִיּ֔וֹן נָ֣טָה קָ֔ו לֹא־הֵשִׁ֥יב יָד֖וֹ מִבַּלֵּ֑עַ וַיַּֽאֲבֶל־חֵ֥ל וְחוֹמָ֖ה יַחְדָּ֥ו אֻמְלָֽלוּ׃ ס [9] טָבְע֤וּ בָאָ֙רֶץ֙ שְׁעָרֶ֔יהָ אִבַּ֥ד וְשִׁבַּ֖ר בְּרִיחֶ֑יהָ מַלְכָּ֤הּ וְשָׂרֶ֙יהָ֙ בַגּוֹיִ֔ם אֵ֣ין תּוֹרָ֔ה גַּם־נְבִיאֶ֕יהָ לֹא־מָצְא֥וּ חָז֖וֹן מֵיְהוָֽה׃ ס

⁷ The Lord has rejected His altar, He has abandoned His sanctuary; He has delivered into the hand of the enemy The walls of her palaces. They have made a noise in the house of the LORD As in the day of an appointed feast.

⁸ The LORD determined to destroy The wall of the daughter of Zion. He has stretched out a line, He has not restrained His hand from destroying, And He has caused rampart and wall to lament; They have languished together.

⁹ Her gates have sunk into the ground, He has destroyed and broken her bars. Her king and her princes are among the nations; The law is no more. Also, her prophets find No vision from the LORD.

¹⁰ The elders of the daughter of Zion Sit on the ground, they are silent. They have thrown dust on their heads; They have girded themselves with sackcloth. The virgins of Jerusalem Have bowed their heads to the ground.

¹¹ My eyes fail because of tears, My spirit is greatly troubled; My heart is poured out on the earth Because of the destruction of the daughter of my people, When little ones and infants faint In the streets of the city.

¹² They say to their mothers, "Where is grain and wine?" As they faint like a wounded man In the streets of the city, As their life is poured out On their mothers' bosom.

¹³ How shall I admonish you? To what shall I compare you, O daughter of Jerusalem? To what shall I liken you as I comfort you, O virgin daughter of Zion? For your ruin is as vast as the sea; Who can heal you?

יֵשְׁב֨וּ לָאָ֤רֶץ יִדְּמוּ֙ זִקְנֵ֣י בַת־צִיּ֔וֹן הֶֽעֱל֤וּ ¹⁰
עָפָר֙ עַל־רֹאשָׁ֔ם חָגְר֖וּ שַׂקִּ֑ים הוֹרִ֤ידוּ
לָאָ֙רֶץ֙ רֹאשָׁ֔ן בְּתוּלֹ֖ת יְרוּשָׁלָֽ͏ִם׃ ס

כָּל֨וּ בַדְּמָע֤וֹת עֵינַי֙ חֳמַרְמְר֣וּ מֵעַ֔י ¹¹
נִשְׁפַּ֤ךְ לָאָ֙רֶץ֙ כְּבֵדִ֔י עַל־שֶׁ֖בֶר בַּת־עַמִּ֑י
בֵּֽעָטֵ֤ף עוֹלֵל֙ וְיוֹנֵ֔ק בִּרְחֹב֖וֹת קִרְיָֽה׃ ס

לְאִמֹּתָם֙ יֹאמְר֔וּ אַיֵּ֖ה דָּגָ֣ן וָיָ֑יִן ¹²
בְּהִֽתְעַטְּפָ֤ם כֶּֽחָלָל֙ בִּרְחֹב֣וֹת עִ֔יר
בְּהִשְׁתַּפֵּ֣ךְ נַפְשָׁ֔ם אֶל־חֵ֖יק אִמֹּתָֽם׃ ס

מָֽה־אֲעִידֵ֞ךְ מָ֣ה אֲדַמֶּה־לָּ֗ךְ הַבַּת֙ ¹³
יְר֣וּשָׁלַ֔͏ִם מָ֤ה אַשְׁוֶה־לָּךְ֙ וַאֲנַֽחֲמֵ֔ךְ
בְּתוּלַ֖ת בַּת־צִיּ֑וֹן כִּֽי־גָד֧וֹל כַּיָּ֛ם שִׁבְרֵ֖ךְ
מִ֥י יִרְפָּא־לָֽךְ׃ ס

נְבִיאַ֗יִךְ חָ֤זוּ לָךְ֙ שָׁ֣וְא וְתָפֵ֔ל וְלֹֽא־גִלּ֥וּ ¹⁴
עַל־עֲוֺנֵ֖ךְ לְהָשִׁ֣יב (שביתך) [שְׁבוּתֵ֑ךְ]
וַיֶּ֣חֱזוּ לָ֔ךְ מַשְׂא֥וֹת שָׁ֖וְא וּמַדּוּחִֽים׃ ס

סָֽפְק֨וּ עָלַ֤יִךְ כַּפַּ֙יִם֙ כָּל־עֹ֣בְרֵי דֶ֔רֶךְ ¹⁵
שָֽׁרְקוּ֙ וַיָּנִ֣עוּ רֹאשָׁ֔ם עַל־בַּ֖ת יְרוּשָׁלָ֑͏ִם
הֲזֹ֣את הָעִ֗יר שֶׁיֹּֽאמְרוּ֙ כְּלִ֣ילַת יֹ֔פִי
מָשׂ֖וֹשׂ לְכָל־הָאָֽרֶץ׃ ס

פָּצ֨וּ עָלַ֤יִךְ פִּיהֶם֙ כָּל־אֹ֣יְבַ֔יִךְ שָֽׁרְקוּ֙ ¹⁶
וַיַּֽחַרְקוּ־שֵׁ֔ן אָמְר֖וּ בִּלָּ֑עְנוּ אַ֣ךְ זֶ֤ה הַיּ֙וֹם
שֶׁקִּוִּינֻ֔הוּ מָצָ֖אנוּ רָאִֽינוּ׃ ס

עָשָׂ֨ה יְהֹוָ֜ה אֲשֶׁ֣ר זָמָ֗ם בִּצַּ֤ע אֶמְרָתוֹ֙ ¹⁷
אֲשֶׁ֣ר צִוָּ֣ה מִֽימֵי־קֶ֔דֶם הָרַ֖ס וְלֹ֣א חָמָ֑ל
וַיְשַׂמַּ֤ח עָלַ֙יִךְ֙ אוֹיֵ֔ב הֵרִ֖ים קֶ֥רֶן צָרָֽיִךְ׃ ס

צָעַ֥ק לִבָּ֖ם אֶל־אֲדֹנָ֑י חוֹמַ֣ת בַּת־צִ֠יּוֹן ¹⁸
הוֹרִ֨ידִי כַנַּ֤חַל דִּמְעָה֙ יוֹמָ֣ם וָלַ֔יְלָה אַֽל־
תִּתְּנִ֤י פוּגַת֙ לָ֔ךְ אַל־תִּדֹּ֖ם בַּת־עֵינֵֽךְ׃ ס

ק֣וּמִי ׀ רֹ֣נִּי (בליל) [בַלַּ֗יְלָה] לְרֹאשׁ֙ ¹⁹
אַשְׁמֻר֔וֹת שִׁפְכִ֤י כַמַּ֙יִם֙ לִבֵּ֔ךְ נֹ֖כַח פְּנֵ֣י
אֲדֹנָ֑י שְׂאִ֧י אֵלָ֣יו כַּפַּ֗יִךְ עַל־נֶ֙פֶשׁ֙ עֽוֹלָלַ֔יִךְ
הָעֲטוּפִ֥ים בְּרָעָ֖ב בְּרֹ֥אשׁ כָּל־חוּצֽוֹת׃ ס

¹⁴ Your prophets have seen for you False and foolish *visions*; And they have not exposed your iniquity So as to restore you from captivity, But they have seen for you false and misleading oracles.

¹⁵ All who pass along the way Clap their hands *in derision* at you; They hiss and shake their heads At the daughter of Jerusalem, "Is this the city of which they said, 'The perfection of beauty, A joy to all the earth '?"

¹⁶ All your enemies Have opened their mouths wide against you; They hiss and gnash *their* teeth. They say, "We have swallowed *her* up! Surely this is the day for which we waited; We have reached *it*, we have seen *it*."

¹⁷ The LORD has done what He purposed; He has accomplished His word Which He commanded from days of old. He has thrown down without sparing, And He has caused the enemy to rejoice over you; He has exalted the might of your adversaries.

¹⁸ Their heart cried out to the Lord, "O wall of the daughter of Zion, Let *your* tears run down like a river day and night; Give yourself no relief, Let your eyes have no rest.

¹⁹ "Arise, cry aloud in the night At the beginning of the night watches; Pour out your heart like water Before the presence of the Lord; Lift up your hands to Him For the life of your little ones Who are faint because of hunger At the head of every street."

²⁰ See, O LORD, and look! With whom have You dealt thus? Should women eat their offspring, The little ones who were born healthy? Should priest and prophet be slain In the sanctuary of the Lord?

²⁰ רְאֵ֤ה יְהוָה֙ וְֽהַבִּ֔יטָה לְמִ֖י עוֹלַ֣לְתָּ כֹּ֑ה אִם־תֹּאכַ֨לְנָה נָשִׁ֤ים פִּרְיָם֙ עֹלְלֵ֣י טִפֻּחִ֔ים אִם־יֵהָרֵ֛ג בְּמִקְדַּ֥שׁ אֲדֹנָ֖י כֹּהֵ֥ן וְנָבִֽיא: ס

²¹ שָׁכְב֨וּ לָאָ֤רֶץ חוּצוֹת֙ נַ֣עַר וְזָקֵ֔ן בְּתוּלֹתַ֥י וּבַחוּרַ֖י נָפְל֣וּ בֶחָ֑רֶב הָרַ֙גְתָּ֙ בְּי֣וֹם אַפֶּ֔ךָ טָבַ֖חְתָּ לֹ֥א חָמָֽלְתָּ: ס

²² תִּקְרָא֩ כְי֨וֹם מוֹעֵ֤ד מְגוּרַי֙ מִסָּבִ֔יב וְלֹ֥א הָיָ֛ה בְּי֥וֹם אַף־יְהוָ֖ה פָּלִ֣יט וְשָׂרִ֑יד אֲשֶׁר־טִפַּ֥חְתִּי וְרִבִּ֖יתִי אֹיְבִ֥י כִלָּֽם: פ

21 On the ground in the streets Lie young and old; My virgins and my young men Have fallen by the sword. You have slain *them* in the day of Your anger, You have slaughtered, not sparing. 22 You called as in the day of an appointed feast My terrors on every side; And there was no one who escaped or survived In the day of the LORD'S anger. Those whom I bore and reared, My enemy annihilated them.	

Process of Discovery

Linguistics Section

Linguistic Structure

A ¹ How the Lord has covered the daughter of Zion With a cloud in His anger! He has cast from Heaven to earth The glory of Israel, And has not remembered His footstool In the day of His anger.

B ² The Lord has swallowed up; He has not spared All the habitations of Jacob. In His wrath He has thrown down The strongholds of the daughter of Judah; He has brought *them* down to the ground; He has profaned the kingdom and its princes.

C ³ In fierce anger He has cut off All the strength of Israel; He has drawn back His right hand From before the enemy. And He has burned in Jacob like a flaming fire Consuming round about.

D ⁴ He has bent His bow like an enemy; He has set His right hand like an adversary And slain all that were pleasant to the eye; In the tent of the daughter of Zion He has poured out His wrath like fire.

E ⁵ The Lord has become like an enemy. He has swallowed up Israel; He has swallowed up all its palaces, He has destroyed its strongholds And multiplied in the daughter of Judah Mourning and moaning.

F ⁶ And He has violently treated His tabernacle like a garden *booth*; He has destroyed His appointed meeting place. The LORD has caused to be forgotten The appointed feast and sabbath in Zion, And He has despised king and priest In the indignation of His anger.

G ⁷ The Lord has rejected His altar, He has abandoned His sanctuary; He has delivered into the hand of the enemy The walls of her palaces. They have made a noise in the house of the LORD As in the day of an appointed feast.

H ⁸ The LORD determined to destroy The wall of the daughter of Zion. He has stretched out a line, He has not restrained His hand from destroying, And He has caused rampart and wall to lament; They have languished together.

I [9] Her gates have sunk into the ground, He has destroyed and broken her bars. Her king and her princes are among the nations; The law is no more. Also, her prophets find No vision from the LORD.

J [10] The elders of the daughter of Zion Sit on the ground, they are silent. They have thrown dust on their heads; They have girded themselves with sackcloth. The virgins of Jerusalem Have bowed their heads to the ground.

K [11] My eyes fail because of tears, My spirit is greatly troubled; My heart is poured out on the earth Because of the destruction of the daughter of my people, When little ones and infants faint In the streets of the city.

K' [12] They say to their mothers, "Where is grain and wine?" As they faint like a wounded man In the streets of the city, As their life is poured out On their mothers' bosom.

J' [13] How shall I admonish you? To what shall I compare you, O daughter of Jerusalem? To what shall I liken you as I comfort you, O virgin daughter of Zion? For your ruin is as vast as the sea; Who can heal you?

I' [14] Your prophets have seen for you False and foolish *visions*; And they have not exposed your iniquity So as to restore you from captivity, But they have seen for you false and misleading oracles.

H' [15] All who pass along the way Clap their hands *in derision* at you; They hiss and shake their heads At the daughter of Jerusalem, "Is this the city of which they said, 'The perfection of beauty, A joy to all the earth '?"

G' [16] All your enemies Have opened their mouths wide against you; They hiss and gnash *their* teeth. They say, "We have swallowed *her* up! Surely this is the day for which we waited; We have reached *it*, we have seen *it*."

F' [17] The LORD has done what He purposed; He has accomplished His word Which He commanded from days of old. He has thrown down without sparing, And He has caused the enemy to rejoice over you; He has exalted the might of your adversaries.

E' [18] Their heart cried out to the Lord, "O wall of the daughter of Zion, Let *your* tears run down like a river day and night; Give yourself no relief, Let your eyes have no rest.

D' [19] "Arise, cry aloud in the night At the beginning of the night watches; Pour out your heart like water Before the presence of the Lord; Lift up your hands to Him For the life of your little ones Who are faint because of hunger At the head of every street."

C' [20] See, O LORD, and look! With whom have You dealt thus? Should women eat their offspring, The little ones who were born healthy? Should priest and prophet be slain In the sanctuary of the Lord?

B' [21] On the ground in the streets Lie young and old; My virgins and my young men Have fallen by the sword. You have slain *them* in the day of Your anger, You have slaughtered, not sparing.

A' [22] You called as in the day of an appointed feast My terrors on every side; And there was no one who escaped or survived In the day of the LORD'S anger. Those whom I bore and reared, My enemy annihilated them.

A: Anger. B: Falling. C: Death of leaders. D: Beloved. E: Girls. F: Leaders. G: Enemies. H: Girls. I: Prophets. J: Girls. K: Infants.[20]

Discussion

Jeremiah describes the destruction of the city of Jerusalem and the Temple. Jeremiah believed that the LORD sent the Babylonian army to punish Israel. When the LORD had sent punishment before Babylon, He never destroyed the country, Jerusalem, or Temple. This time was different. The transgressions of idolatry showed the LORD that the people of Judah did not believe and did not want to follow the Laws of the Torah. Since the treaty between the people and

---

[20] Hajime Murai, "Literary Structure (Chiasm, Chiasmus) of Book of Lamentations," Literary structure (chiasm, chiasmus) of each pericopes of Book of Lamentations, accessed April 21, 2020, http://www.bible.literarystructure.info/bible/25_Lamentations_pericope_e.html.

the LORD was broken, the LORD's protection was gone. From the theologian's point of view, it was the LORD sending punishment instead of the LORD removing His protection on that day.

Questioning the Passage

1. What is the LORD's footstool? (v. 2)

    The LORD's footstool is the Temple in Jerusalem. The daughter of Zion is Jerusalem.

2. What does it mean that "the LORD has swallowed up" in verse two?

    In this context, the LORD destroyed Jerusalem and the Temple. Theologians in the days of the Babylonian Exile believed that the LORD sent the Babylonians to punish the people for their transgressions. The Temple was overrun with pagans, and the holy vessels were taken to Babylon.

    The Targum says that the LORD had destroyed the land and its buildings without mercy. The LORD leveled everything to the ground and, in doing so, desecrated the kingdom.[21]

3. What does it mean that the LORD bent his bow like an enemy? (v. 4)

    When an archer prepares to fire his arrow, he uses his feet to help him to pull the bow back. Jeremiah saw the LORD as being one of the Babylonian archers. They bent their bows to fire their arrows into the city of Jerusalem.[22]

---

[21] Martin McNamara, Kevin J. Cathcart, and Michael Maher, *The Aramaic Bible: the Targums* (Wilmington, DE: M. Glazier, 1987).

[22] Zlotowitz, Meir, and Nosson Scherman. *Megillas Eichah = Lamentations: A New Translation with a Commentary Anthologized from Talmudic, Midrashic and Rabbinic Sources*. New York: Mesorah Publications, 1979. N. pag. Print.

4. What is a garden booth? (v. 6)

A garden booth is nothing more than a mere garden. It is easy to pull up a garden, thus leaving the soil barren. In the same way, the LORD "pulled up" His house.

5. What were the rampart and the wall in verse eight?

The rampart was a lower wall constructed outside the high city walls. The verse implies that the LORD only wanted the walls of Jerusalem to be destroyed. He did not want the ramparts (the lower wall) destroyed. Once the siege began, nothing was sacred nor safe from destruction.[23] Was it essential that the entire city and Temple be destroyed for the LORD to tell Israel that the LORD was angry with them? The destruction may not have been the ultimate goal. A remanent of the people was taken from the land and would be restored seventy years later.

6. What is occurring in verse nine?

The Targum says that a pig was slaughtered, and its blood was upon the people. The pig is an unclean animal and is forbidden to eat. The pig symbolizes the sins of the people. The sins were idolatry and not following the Laws of the Torah. The Kosher laws are a part of the Torah.

7. Why were the elders silent? (v. 10)

The elders were done trying to tell the people to repent from their sins. It was too late. Why continue lecturing people about their sinfulness when the city's walls were breached? The enemies of Israel and the LORD were in the Temple. The road to repentance took a different course.

---

[23] IBID.

8. What does "my heart is poured out on the earth" mean? (v. 11)

   Jeremiah was talking about the honor and pride of the nation that had been trampled by the enemies of Judah. The beautiful city and Temple, which was the pride of Judah, were gone.[24]

9. Where were the grain and wind? (v. 12)

   There was a famine in the city of Jerusalem during the siege. Many residents of the city died of starvation. Food was grown outside the city walls. The army surrounding the city took the food from the fields.

10. What does it mean that Judah's ruin was as vast as the sea? (v. 13)

    The destruction of Judah was so massive that it could not be repaired by natural means. It was going to take an act of the LORD to recover the nation, Jerusalem, and the Temple.[25]

11. What is verse sixteen referring to?

    The day that Jeremiah is referring to is the ninth day of Av. Arizal[iii] believed that the LORD sent fire down upon the Temple before the invading army could reach the Temple. Thus, the LORD destroyed His own Temple. He would not allow the pagans to see the LORD's house desecrated.[26]

---

[24] Lamsa, George M., Rocco Errico A. "Lamentations Chapter 1." In *Aramaic Light on Isaiah, Jeremiah, and Lamentations*, by Smyrna: Noorah, 2011

[25] Zlotowitz, Meir, and Nosson Scherman. "Chapter 1." *Megillas Eichah = Lamentations: A New Translation with a Commentary Anthologized from Talmudic, Midrashic and Rabbinic Sources*. New York: Mesorah Publications, 1979. N. pag. Print.

[26] IBID.

12. What does the phrase "Let your eyes have no rest" mean? (v. 18)

The Jewish people were instructed by Jeremiah to remember the day the Temple of the LORD was destroyed. The sins of the people, especially their princes, led the people into sin.[27]

13. What does verse nineteen mean?

The Targum says that the people needed to return to their daily prayers. Three times a day, morning, afternoon, and evening prayer was held. "Lift up your hands to Him" means that the people needed to call upon the Shekinah to return and protect them.[28] In this period, people believed that the Shekinah was with the people. In the book of Ezekiel, the prophet describes the day that Shekinah left the Temple.

14. Did cannibalism occur in Jerusalem? (v. 20)

The thought of a mother or father eating their children to survive a famine is unthinkable and revolting. This verse says that the famine got so bad that the people almost resorted to cannibalism. The princes of Jerusalem knew that the famine had gotten that bad. Instead of surrendering, the princes (King included) tried to escape the city. Most of them were captured. How could the leaders of Jerusalem allow the starvation and suffering of the people? They probably prayed to their idols and awaited salvation from them. A lesson from this event is that idols are false gods and will never be able to help people because they do not exist.

---

[27] IBID.

[28] Martin McNamara, Kevin J. Cathcart, and Michael Maher, *The Aramaic Bible: the Targums* (Wilmington, DE: M. Glazier, 1987).

15. What is the day of the appointed feast? (v. 22)

The Targum says that the appointed feast will come when the people are given their freedom at the hands of the Messiah in the same way that Moses offered freedom at the first Passover. The later part of the verse says that Judah's army was destroyed.[29]

Phrase Study

1. בָּלַע *(bala')* II, *confuse, confound.* (v. 5)

"Used of men (Isa 28:4), fish (Jon 2:1), serpent (Ex 7:12), and animals (Gen 41:7, 24). On two different occasions, the Lord cause the earth to open and swallow alive groups men as a judgment: at the Red Sea (Ex 15:12) and at the Korah, Dathan, and Abiram rebellion (Num 16:30, 32, 34; 26:10; Deut 11:6; and Ps 106:17). Frequently the word is used as a symbol of destruction and ruin: Lam 2:2, 5, 8; Isa 3:12; 49:19; etc."[30]

2. (v. 3) כֹּל קֶרֶן יִשְׂרָאֵל

This phrase is translated in the Midrash and Targum as "the dignity of Israel." The middle word of the phrase means "horns." When Moses came down from Mount Sinai, he had "horns" coming off his face. The "horns" were not horns but rather the dignity of Israel, who accepted the LORD's Torah. The New American Standard 1995 Bible translates this phrase as "the strength of Israel." The dignity and strength of Israel came from following the Laws of the LORD. That dignity was gone.

---

[29] IBID.
[30] Robert Laird. Harris, *Theological Word Book of the Old Testament*, 1981.

Thoughts

The darkest day in Jewish history is the ninth day of Av. On this day, the Temple at Jerusalem was destroyed along with the city of Jerusalem. According to Jeremiah, the destruction would have been avoided if the people had turned away from idolatry and sin. Sounds simple, right? It may have been simple, but it was not done. It is equated to a bad habit, i.e., smoking cigarettes. Once addicted, it is difficult to drop the habit. Sin gives a person a mental high that feels good. Even if the person knows that what is being done is morally or ethically wrong, they still do it. A warning from the ninth day of Av is that one must avoid sin at all costs. Eventually, payment needs to be made for sin. It may not be in this life. However, it will affect the world to come.

Michael Harvey Koplitz

Chapter Three

Language

New American Standard 1995	Hebrew
[1] I am the man who has seen affliction Because of the rod of His wrath.	אֲנִי הַגֶּבֶר רָאָה עֳנִי בְּשֵׁבֶט עֶבְרָתוֹ: [2]
[2] He has driven me and made me walk In darkness and not in light.	אוֹתִי נָהַג וַיֹּלַךְ חֹשֶׁךְ וְלֹא־אוֹר:
[3] Surely against me He has turned His hand Repeatedly all the day.	אַךְ בִּי יָשֻׁב יַהֲפֹךְ יָדוֹ כָּל־הַיּוֹם: ס [3]
[4] He has caused my flesh and my skin to waste away, He has broken my bones.	בִּלָּה בְשָׂרִי וְעוֹרִי שִׁבַּר עַצְמוֹתָי: [4]
[5] He has besieged and encompassed me with bitterness and hardship.	בָּנָה עָלַי וַיַּקַּף רֹאשׁ וּתְלָאָה: [5]
[6] In dark places He has made me dwell, Like those who have long been dead.	בְּמַחֲשַׁכִּים הוֹשִׁיבַנִי כְּמֵתֵי עוֹלָם: ס [6]
[7] He has walled me in so that I cannot go out; He has made my chain heavy.	גָּדַר בַּעֲדִי וְלֹא אֵצֵא הִכְבִּיד נְחָשְׁתִּי: [7]
[8] Even when I cry out and call for help, He shuts out my prayer.	גַּם כִּי אֶזְעַק וַאֲשַׁוֵּעַ שָׂתַם תְּפִלָּתִי: [8]
[9] He has blocked my ways with hewn stone; He has made my paths crooked.	גָּדַר דְּרָכַי בְּגָזִית נְתִיבֹתַי עִוָּה: ס [9]
[10] He is to me like a bear lying in wait, *Like* a lion in secret places.	דֹּב אֹרֵב הוּא לִי (אַרְיֵה) [אֲרִי] [10] בְּמִסְתָּרִים:
[11] He has turned aside my ways and torn me to pieces; He has made me desolate.	דְּרָכַי סוֹרֵר וַיְפַשְּׁחֵנִי שָׂמַנִי שֹׁמֵם: [11]
[12] He bent His bow And set me as a target for the arrow.	דָּרַךְ קַשְׁתּוֹ וַיַּצִּיבֵנִי כַּמַּטָּרָא לַחֵץ: ס [12]
[13] He made the arrows of His quiver To enter into my inward parts.	הֵבִיא בְּכִלְיוֹתָי בְּנֵי אַשְׁפָּתוֹ: [13]
[14] I have become a laughingstock to all my people, Their *mocking* song all the day.	הָיִיתִי שְּׂחֹק לְכָל־עַמִּי נְגִינָתָם כָּל־הַיּוֹם: [14]
[15] He has filled me with bitterness, He has made me drunk with wormwood.	הִשְׂבִּיעַנִי בַמְּרוֹרִים הִרְוַנִי לַעֲנָה: ס [15]
	וַיַּגְרֵס בֶּחָצָץ שִׁנָּי הִכְפִּישַׁנִי בָּאֵפֶר: [16]
	וַתִּזְנַח מִשָּׁלוֹם נַפְשִׁי נָשִׁיתִי טוֹבָה: [17]
	וָאֹמַר אָבַד נִצְחִי וְתוֹחַלְתִּי מֵיהוָה: ס [18]
	זְכָר־עָנְיִי וּמְרוּדִי לַעֲנָה וָרֹאשׁ: [19]
	זָכוֹר תִּזְכּוֹר (וְתָשִׁיחַ) [וְתָשׁוֹחַ] עָלַי [20] נַפְשִׁי:
	זֹאת אָשִׁיב אֶל־לִבִּי עַל־כֵּן אוֹחִיל: ס [21]

¹⁶ He has broken my teeth with gravel; He has made me cower in the dust.

¹⁷ My soul has been rejected from peace; I have forgotten happiness.

¹⁸ So I say, "My strength has perished, And *so has* my hope from the LORD."

¹⁹ Remember my affliction and my wandering, the wormwood and bitterness.

²⁰ Surely my soul remembers And is bowed down within me.

²¹ This I recall to my mind, Therefore I have hope.

²² The LORD'S lovingkindnesses indeed never cease, For His compassions never fail.

²³ *They* are new every morning; Great is Your faithfulness.

²⁴ "The LORD is my portion," says my soul, "Therefore I have hope in Him."

²⁵ The LORD is good to those who wait for Him, To the person who seeks Him.

²⁶ *It is* good that he waits silently For the salvation of the LORD.

²⁷ *It is* good for a man that he should bear The yoke in his youth.

²⁸ Let him sit alone and be silent Since He has laid *it* on him.

²⁹ Let him put his mouth in the dust, Perhaps there is hope.

³⁰ Let him give his cheek to the smiter, Let him be filled with reproach.

³¹ For the Lord will not reject forever,

³² For if He causes grief, Then He will have compassion According to His abundant lovingkindness.

³³ For He does not afflict willingly Or grieve the sons of men.

³⁴ To crush under His feet All the prisoners of the land,

---

22 חַסְדֵי יְהוָה כִּי לֹא־תָמְנוּ כִּי לֹא־כָלוּ רַחֲמָיו:

23 חֲדָשִׁים לַבְּקָרִים רַבָּה אֱמוּנָתֶךָ:

24 חֶלְקִי יְהוָה אָמְרָה נַפְשִׁי עַל־כֵּן אוֹחִיל לוֹ: ס

25 טוֹב יְהוָה לְקֹוָו לְנֶפֶשׁ תִּדְרְשֶׁנּוּ:

26 טוֹב וְיָחִיל וְדוּמָם לִתְשׁוּעַת יְהוָה:

27 טוֹב לַגֶּבֶר כִּי־יִשָּׂא עֹל בִּנְעוּרָיו: ס

28 יֵשֵׁב בָּדָד וְיִדֹּם כִּי נָטַל עָלָיו:

29 יִתֵּן בֶּעָפָר פִּיהוּ אוּלַי יֵשׁ תִּקְוָה:

30 יִתֵּן לְמַכֵּהוּ לֶחִי יִשְׂבַּע בְּחֶרְפָּה: ס

31 כִּי לֹא יִזְנַח לְעוֹלָם אֲדֹנָי:

32 כִּי אִם־הוֹגָה וְרִחַם כְּרֹב (חַסְדּוֹ) [חֲסָדָיו]:

33 כִּי לֹא עִנָּה מִלִּבּוֹ וַיַּגֶּה בְּנֵי־אִישׁ: ס

34 לְדַכֵּא תַּחַת רַגְלָיו כֹּל אֲסִירֵי אָרֶץ:

35 לְהַטּוֹת מִשְׁפַּט־גָּבֶר נֶגֶד פְּנֵי עֶלְיוֹן:

36 לְעַוֵּת אָדָם בְּרִיבוֹ אֲדֹנָי לֹא רָאָה: ס

37 מִי זֶה אָמַר וַתֶּהִי אֲדֹנָי לֹא צִוָּה:

38 מִפִּי עֶלְיוֹן לֹא תֵצֵא הָרָעוֹת וְהַטּוֹב:

39 מַה־יִּתְאוֹנֵן אָדָם חָי גֶּבֶר עַל־(חֶטְאוֹ) [חֲטָאָיו]: ס

40 נַחְפְּשָׂה דְרָכֵינוּ וְנַחְקֹרָה וְנָשׁוּבָה עַד־יְהוָה:

41 נִשָּׂא לְבָבֵנוּ אֶל־כַּפָּיִם אֶל־אֵל בַּשָּׁמָיִם:

42 נַחְנוּ פָשַׁעְנוּ וּמָרִינוּ אַתָּה לֹא סָלָחְתָּ: ס

43 סַכֹּתָה בָאַף וַתִּרְדְּפֵנוּ הָרַגְתָּ לֹא חָמָלְתָּ:

44 סַכּוֹתָה בֶעָנָן לָךְ מֵעֲבוֹר תְּפִלָּה:

45 סְחִי וּמָאוֹס תְּשִׂימֵנוּ בְּקֶרֶב הָעַמִּים: ס

46 פָּצוּ עָלֵינוּ פִּיהֶם כָּל־אֹיְבֵינוּ:

35 To deprive a man of justice In the presence of the Most High,

36 To defraud a man in his lawsuit-- Of these things the Lord does not approve.

37 Who is there who speaks and it comes to pass, Unless the Lord has commanded *it*?

38 *Is it* not from the mouth of the Most High That both good and ill go forth?

39 Why should *any* living mortal, or *any* man, Offer complaint in view of his sins?

40 Let us examine and probe our ways, And let us return to the LORD.

41 We lift up our heart and hands Toward God in Heaven;

42 We have transgressed and rebelled, You have not pardoned.

43 You have covered *Yourself* with anger And pursued us; You have slain *and* have not spared.

44 You have covered Yourself with a cloud So that no prayer can pass through.

45 *You have made us mere* offscouring and refuse In the midst of the peoples.

46 All our enemies have opened their mouths against us.

47 Panic and pitfall have befallen us, Devastation and destruction;

48 My eyes run down with streams of water Because of the destruction of the daughter of my people.

49 My eyes pour down unceasingly, Without stopping,

50 Until the LORD looks down And sees from Heaven.

51 My eyes bring pain to my soul Because of all the daughters of my city.

52 My enemies without cause Hunted me down like a bird;

53 They have silenced me in the pit And have placed a stone on me.

פַּחַד וָפַחַת הָיָה לָנוּ הַשֵּׁאת וְהַשָּׁבֶר: 47

פַּלְגֵי־מַיִם֙ תֵּרַד עֵינִ֔י עַל־שֶׁבֶר בַּת־ 48
עַמִּי: ס

עֵינִי נִגְּרָה וְלֹא תִדְמֶה מֵאֵין הֲפֻגוֹת: 49

עַד־יַשְׁקִיף וְיֵרֶא יְהוָה מִשָּׁמָיִם: 50

עֵינִי֙ עוֹלְלָה לְנַפְשִׁי מִכֹּל בְּנוֹת עִירִי: 51

ס

צוֹד צָדוּנִי כַּצִּפּוֹר אֹיְבַי חִנָּם: 52

צָמְתוּ בַבּוֹר֙ חַיָּ֔י וַיַּדּוּ־אֶבֶן בִּי: 53

צָפוּ־מַיִם עַל־רֹאשִׁי אָמַרְתִּי נִגְזָרְתִּי: 54

ס

קָרָאתִי שִׁמְךָ֙ יְהוָ֔ה מִבּוֹר תַּחְתִּיּוֹת: 55

קוֹלִי שָׁמָעְתָּ אַל־תַּעְלֵם אָזְנְךָ֛ 56
לְרַוְחָתִי לְשַׁוְעָתִי:

קָרַ֙בְתָּ֙ בְּיוֹם אֶקְרָאֶ֔ךָּ אָמַרְתָּ אַל־ 57
תִּירָא: ס

רַבְתָּ אֲדֹנָי רִיבֵי נַפְשִׁי גָּאַלְתָּ חַיָּי: 58

רָאִיתָה יְהוָה֙ עַוָּתָתִ֔י שָׁפְטָה 59
מִשְׁפָּטִי:

רָאִיתָה֙ כָּל־נִקְמָתָ֔ם כָּל־מַחְשְׁבֹתָם 60
לִי: ס

שָׁמַעְתָּ חֶרְפָּתָם֙ יְהוָ֔ה כָּל־מַחְשְׁבֹתָם 61
עָלָי:

שִׂפְתֵי קָמַי֙ וְהֶגְיוֹנָ֔ם עָלַי כָּל־הַיּוֹם: 62

שִׁבְתָּם וְקִימָתָם֙ הַבִּיטָה אֲנִי 63
מַנְגִּינָתָם: ס

תָּשִׁיב לָהֶם גְּמוּל יְהוָה כְּמַעֲשֵׂה 64
יְדֵיהֶם:

תִּתֵּן לָהֶם מְגִנַּת־לֵב תַּאֲלָתְךָ לָהֶם: 65

תִּרְדֹּף בְּאַף֙ וְתַשְׁמִידֵ֔ם מִתַּחַת שְׁמֵי 66
יְהוָה: פ

⁵⁴ Waters flowed over my head; I said, "I am cut off!"

⁵⁵ I called on Your name, O LORD, Out of the lowest pit.

⁵⁶ You have heard my voice, "Do not hide Your ear from my *prayer for* relief, From my cry for help."

⁵⁷ You drew near when I called on You; You said, "Do not fear!"

⁵⁸ O Lord, You have pleaded my soul's cause; You have redeemed my life.

⁵⁹ O LORD, You have seen my oppression; Judge my case.

⁶⁰ You have seen all their vengeance, All their schemes against me.

⁶¹ You have heard their reproach, O LORD, All their schemes against me.

⁶² The lips of my assailants and their whispering *Are* against me all day long.

⁶³ Look on their sitting and their rising; I am their mocking song.

⁶⁴ You will recompense them, O LORD, According to the work of their hands.

⁶⁵ You will give them hardness of heart, Your curse will be on them.

⁶⁶ You will pursue them in anger and destroy them From under the heavens of the LORD!

Process of Discovery

Linguistics Section

Linguistic Structure

A [1] I am the man who has seen affliction Because of the rod of His wrath. [2] He has driven me and made me walk In darkness and not in light. [3] Surely against me He has turned His hand Repeatedly all the day.

B [4] He has caused my flesh and my skin to waste away, He has broken my bones. [5] He has besieged and encompassed me with bitterness and hardship. [6] In dark places He has made me dwell, Like those who have long been dead.

C [7] He has walled me in so that I cannot go out; He has made my chain heavy. [8] Even when I cry out and call for help, He shuts out my prayer. [9] He has blocked my ways with hewn stone; He has made my paths crooked.

D [10] He is to me like a bear lying in wait, *Like* a lion in secret places. [11] He has turned aside my ways and torn me to pieces; He has made me desolate. [12] He bent His bow And set me as a target for the arrow.

E [13] He made the arrows of His quiver To enter into my inward parts. [14] I have become a laughingstock to all my people, Their *mocking* song all the day. [15] He has filled me with bitterness, He has made me drunk with wormwood.

F [16] He has broken my teeth with gravel; He has made me cower in the dust. [17] My soul has been rejected from peace; I have forgotten happiness. [18] So I say, "My strength has perished, And *so has* my hope from the LORD."

G [19] Remember my affliction and my wandering, the wormwood and bitterness. [20] Surely my soul remembers And is bowed down within me. [21] This I recall to my mind, Therefore I have hope.

H [22] The LORD'S lovingkindnesses indeed never cease, For His compassions never fail. [23] *They* are new every morning; Great is Your faithfulness. [24] "The LORD is my portion," says my soul, "Therefore I have hope in Him."

I [25] The LORD is good to those who wait for Him, To the person who seeks Him. [26] *It is* good that he waits silently For the salvation of the LORD. [27] *It is* good for a man that he should bear The yoke in his youth.

J [28] Let him sit alone and be silent Since He has laid *it* on him.[29] Let him put his mouth in the dust, Perhaps there is hope. [30] Let him give his cheek to the smiter, Let him be filled with reproach.

K [31] For the Lord will not reject forever, [32] For if He causes grief, Then He will have compassion According to His abundant lovingkindness. [33] For He does not afflict willingly Or grieve the sons of men.

K' [34] To crush under His feet All the prisoners of the land, [35] To deprive a man of justice In the presence of the Most High, [36] To defraud a man in his lawsuit-- Of these things the Lord does not approve.

J' [37] Who is there who speaks and it comes to pass, Unless the Lord has commanded *it*? [38] *Is it* not from the mouth of the Most High That both good and ill go forth? [39] Why should *any* living mortal, or *any* man, Offer complaint in view of his sins?

I' [40] Let us examine and probe our ways, And let us return to the LORD. [41] We lift up our heart and hands Toward God in Heaven; [42] We have transgressed and rebelled, You have not pardoned.

H' [43] You have covered *Yourself* with anger And pursued us; You have slain *and* have not spared. [44] You have covered Yourself with a cloud So that no prayer can pass through. [45] *You have made us mere* offscouring and refuse In the midst of the peoples.

G' [46] All our enemies have opened their mouths against us. [47] Panic and pitfall have befallen us, Devastation and destruction; [48] My eyes run down with streams of water Because of the destruction of the daughter of my people.

F' [49] My eyes pour down unceasingly, Without stopping, [50] Until the LORD looks down And sees from Heaven. [51] My eyes bring pain to my soul Because of all the daughters of my city.

E' [52] My enemies without cause Hunted me down like a bird; [53] They have silenced me in the pit And have placed a stone on me. [54] Waters flowed over my head; I said, "I am cut off!"

D' [55] I called on Your name, O LORD, Out of the lowest pit. [56] You have heard my voice, "Do not hide Your ear from my *prayer for* relief, From my cry for help." [57] You drew near when I called on You; You said, "Do not fear!"

C' [58] O Lord, You have pleaded my soul's cause; You have redeemed my life. [59] O LORD, You have seen my oppression; Judge my case. [60] You have seen all their vengeance, All their schemes against me.

B' [61] You have heard their reproach, O LORD, All their schemes against me. [62] The lips of my assailants and their whispering *Are* against me all day long. [63] Look on their sitting and their rising; I am their mocking song.

A' [64] You will recompense them, O LORD, According to the work of their hands. [65] You will give them hardness of heart, Your curse will be on them. [66] You will pursue them in anger and destroy them From under the heavens of the LORD!

A: Anger. B: Sufferings. C: Wishing for salvation. D: Predicament. E: Attacks. F: Waiting for salvation. G: Sufferings. H: Judgement. I: Calling to the LORD. J: To endure hardships. K: The LORD doesn't forsake.[31]

Discussion

This chapter is a very dense chiasm of emotions.

Questioning the Passage

1. Whose anger is referred to in verse one?

   The New American Standard 1995 Bible inserts the pronoun "His," indicating that it is the LORD's anger. The Targum also says that this is the LORD's anger. The rod is usually a symbol of love and peace. The Targum reluctantly

---

[31] Hajime Murai, "Literary Structure (Chiasm, Chiasmus) of Book of Lamentations," Literary structure (chiasm, chiasmus) of each pericopes of Book of Lamentations, accessed April 21, 2020, http://www.bible.literarystructure.info/bible/25_Lamentations_pericope_e.html.

translates the rod of anger as being from the LORD. It is not the rod that should be examined but rather whose anger is being discussed.[32]

2. What does it mean that the LORD has "turned his hand repeatedly all the day?" (v. 3)

    This means that the LORD wanted the punishment of Judah to be constant.[33] The Exile was a punishment that the people would not forget nor be forgiven until seventy years had passed. They did not feel the LORD's compassion for His people until the end of the Exile.

3. What does verse four mean?

    The LORD wanted the pain of the Exile to be intense. The skin and flesh are sensitive to pain. The bones do not feel pain unless they are broken. The people felt the torture of the punishment for their sins.

4. What is the bitterness and hardship expressed in verse five?

    This is a reference to the Exile. The people suffered from the famine, which overtook Jerusalem when the Babylonian army sieged the city. Then the people watched as the Babylonian army broke through the city walls. The invaders killed many of Jerusalem's inhabitants. The city was torched. The Temple was raided and burnt to the ground.

---

[32] Martin McNamara, Kevin J. Cathcart, and Michael Maher, *The Aramaic Bible: the Targums* (Wilmington, DE: M. Glazier, 1987).

[33] Zlotowitz, Meir, and Nosson Scherman. "Chapter 1." *Megillas Eichah = Lamentations: A New Translation with a Commentary Anthologized from Talmudic, Midrashic and Rabbinic Sources*. New York: Mesorah Publications, 1979. N. pag. Print.

5. What are the dark places in verse six?

   The dark places were in the Babylonian Empire. The people still believed that the LORD could only be sensed inside the borders of Judah. They did not know that the LORD would be with them in Babylon.

6. What does it mean to be walled in? (v. 7)

   To be walled in refers to Exile. The people were placed in communities inside the Empire and not allowed to travel. Once in Babylon, the people could not travel back to Judah or Jerusalem.

7. What does verse twelve mean?

   The order is reversed in verse twelve. The archer would first set himself to target his enemy. Then he would bend his bow. Finally, he would shoot. In this verse, the archer does it in reverse. The Sefer Lechem Dim' ah[iv] (book of Bread and Tears) says that this verse implies that the enemy of Israel kept the people in constant terror because his bow was ready to strike.[34]

8. What does it mean that "he has broken my teeth with gravel?" (v. 16)

   The Sage Rashi said that because the people had to make their bread in the pits dug into the ground, it was mixed from grit and dirt when they kneaded the bread. If a person chewed hard on a small stone, their teeth could be broken.[35]

---

[34] IBID.

[35] Zlotowitz, Meir, and Nosson Scherman. "Chapter 3." *Megillas Eichah = Lamentations: A New Translation with a Commentary Anthologized from Talmudic, Midrashic and Rabbinic Sources*. New York: Mesorah Publications, 1979. N. pag. Print.

9. What does verse seventeen mean?

   The Targum reads, "And my soul shrank from asking for peace; I forgot prosperity."[36] Jeremiah stopped praying for the invasion to stop. Peace with Babylon was not going to happen in a way that was profitable to the Judeans. The Babylonian army took the property of the Jews. Prosperity did not happen again for many years.

10. What does "he puts his mouth in the dust" mean? (v. 29)

    After verse twenty, the chapter's emphasis changed from lamenting to showing faith in the LORD's love. This phrase is an Aramaic idiom: "He does not boast or speak of great things."[37] The people who were taken into Exile suffered because of the sins of their parents and the generations before who violated the LORD's Torah. Judah's leaders, kings, and princes led the people astray to the point that the LORD stepped in. During the time of the destruction of the Temple, the LORD did not speak to the people.

    The Sages' interpretation is that the people needed to repent of their sins.[38]

11. What does the phrase "to crush under his feet" mean? (v. 34)

    The Targum says in verse thirty-four that this phrase means "to humble and subdue beneath his feet."[39]

---

[36] Martin McNamara, Kevin J. Cathcart, and Michael Maher, *The Aramaic Bible: the Targums* (Wilmington, DE: M. Glazier, 1987).

[37] Lamsa, George M., Rocco Errico A. "Lamentations Chapter 1." In *Aramaic Light on Isaiah, Jeremiah, and Lamentations*, by Smyrna: Noorah, 2011

[38] Zlotowitz, Meir, and Nosson Scherman. "Chapter 3." *Megillas Eichah = Lamentations: A New Translation with a Commentary Anthologized from Talmudic, Midrashic and Rabbinic Sources*. New York: Mesorah Publications, 1979. N. pag. Print.

[39] Martin McNamara, Kevin J. Cathcart, and Michael Maher, *The Aramaic Bible: the Targums* (Wilmington, DE: M. Glazier, 1987).

12. What does verse thirty-nine mean?

The Targum offers the following, "What profit shall a person find who sins all the days of his life, a wicked man for his sins?"[40] The sins may give a person some power and wealth, but in the long term, the person will suffer for their sins, especially in the world to come.

13. What does verse forty-five mean?

The Targum translates this verse as "Wanderers and vagabonds you have made us among the nations."[41] The Jewish people were a people without a country. The nation was forced to live in areas of the Babylonian Empire where it was clear they did not belong. It is the beginning of the creation of the Diaspora. The people were scattered, and thus reforming the nation was difficult.

Phrase Study

1. חֹשֶׁךְ וְלֹא־אוֹר (v. 2) – this is a darkness to which there is no hope for light. Darkness is evil, while the light is the LORD.

2. נְתִיבֹתַי עִוָּה (v. 9) – tangled or crooked path. The Israelites knew that even if they escaped captivity, they would be caught on any road they traveled. The Babylonian soldiers lined the way looking for escaped prisoners. The crooked path can refer to a Jewish traveler trying to avoid captivity. It would have been not easy because the traveler could not use normal pathways.[42]

---

[40] IBID.

[41] IBID.

[42] Robert Laird. Harris, *Theological Word Book of the Old Testament*, 1981.

Culture Section

Questioning the passage

1. What does "let him give his cheek to the smiter" mean? (v. 30)

   This saying is an expression in the Near East that means "turn the other cheek" today. Weak and conquered people are usually wounded or killed when they strike back against their oppressors. To turn the other cheek means to accept the lesser evil. It is better to be oppressed than dead.

   Near Eastern people who were defeated would be reproached and struck on their cheeks. The victim would never strike back, allowing the LORD to take care of any revenge.[43]

   Yeshua said in Matthew 5:39, "But I say to you, do not resist an evil person; but ᵃwhoever slaps you on your right cheek, turn the other to him also." Lamentations 3:30 is an echo of what Yeshua said. Yeshua tells us that when a person or nation is wronged by an enemy, the person must not take action. Instead, the person must place trust that the LORD will take care of things and make things right.

2. What does "My eyes run down with streams of water" mean? (v. 48)

   This is a Near Eastern idiom that means "I weep bitterly." It is not meant to be read literally. Near Eastern people often say, "rivers of water run down my eyes."[44]

---

[43] Lamsa, George M., Rocco Errico A. "Lamentations Chapter 1." In *Aramaic Light on Isaiah, Jeremiah, and Lamentations*, by Smyrna: Noorah, 2011
[44] IBID.

3. What does "water flowed over my head" mean? (v. 54)

    This phrase means, "I was surrounded by all kinds of difficulties." In the Near East, when a man is in trouble, he says, "I am sunk in the water." This means that he is in trouble.[45] The people of Judah were in trouble. The Babylonians destroyed their land, cities, and Temple and exiled them from their land.

4. What does peoples' sitting down and standing up mean in verse sixty-three?

    This Near Eastern idiom refers to a person's conduct, etiquette, and manners.[46]

Thoughts

The chapter commences with an examination of why the LORD abandoned His chosen people. The people of Judah brought the Babylonian army upon themselves because they had turned away from the LORD's way. This is what the author is saying. In the time of Jeremiah, the people believed that everything was done because of the will of the LORD. It is a theological way of analyzing what was happening. About halfway through the chapter, Jeremiah turns back to the LORD and offers the LORD praise. Even in bad times, the people must be reminded that the LORD still loves them. We would call what the LORD did to His people "tough love." Parents understand that there are times a parent(s) must refuse a demand made by a child for their own good. The people of Judah may not have fully understood why the sky was falling upon them. It was more important to remember that the LORD was still with His people.

---

[45] IBID.
[46] IBID.

Michael Harvey Koplitz

New American Standard 1995	Hebrew

New American Standard 1995

[1] How dark the gold has become, *How* the pure gold has changed! The sacred stones are poured out At the corner of every street.

[2] The precious sons of Zion, Weighed against fine gold, How they are regarded as earthen jars, The work of a potter's hands!

[3] Even jackals offer the breast, They nurse their young; *But* the daughter of my people has become cruel Like ostriches in the wilderness.

[4] The tongue of the infant cleaves To the roof of its mouth because of thirst; The little ones ask for bread, *But* no one breaks *it* for them.

[5] Those who ate delicacies Are desolate in the streets; Those reared in purple Embrace ash pits.

[6] For the iniquity of the daughter of my people Is greater than the sin of Sodom, Which was overthrown as in a moment, And no hands were turned toward her.

[7] Her consecrated ones were purer than snow, They were whiter than milk; They were more ruddy *in* body than corals, Their polishing *was like* lapis lazuli.

[8] Their appearance is blacker than soot, They are not recognized in the streets; Their skin is shriveled on their bones, It is withered, it has become like wood.

[9] Better are those slain with the sword Than those slain with hunger; For they

Hebrew

אֵיכָה֙ יוּעַם֙ זָהָ֔ב יִשְׁנֶ֖א הַכֶּ֣תֶם הַטֹּ֑וב תִּשְׁתַּפֵּ֙כְנָה֙ אַבְנֵי־קֹ֔דֶשׁ בְּרֹ֖אשׁ כָּל־חוּצֹֽות׃ ס

[2] בְּנֵ֤י צִיֹּון֙ הַיְקָרִ֔ים הַמְסֻלָּאִ֖ים בַּפָּ֑ז אֵיכָ֤ה נֶחְשְׁבוּ֙ לְנִבְלֵי־חֶ֔רֶשׂ מַעֲשֵׂ֖ה יְדֵ֥י יוֹצֵֽר׃ ס

[3] גַּם־(תַּנִּין) [תַּנִּים֙] חָ֣לְצוּ שַׁ֔ד הֵינִ֖יקוּ גּוּרֵיהֶ֑ן בַּת־עַמִּ֣י לְאַכְזָ֔ר (כִּי) (עֵנִים) [כַּיְעֵנִ֖ים] בַּמִּדְבָּֽר׃ ס

[4] דָּבַ֨ק לְשֹׁ֥ון יֹונֵ֛ק אֶל־חִכֹּ֖ו בַּצָּמָ֑א עֹֽולָלִים֙ שָׁ֣אֲלוּ לֶ֔חֶם פֹּרֵ֖שׂ אֵ֥ין לָהֶֽם׃ ס

[5] הָאֹֽכְלִים֙ לְמַ֣עֲדַנִּ֔ים נָשַׁ֖מּוּ בַּחוּצֹ֑ות הָאֱמֻנִים֙ עֲלֵ֣י תֹולָ֔ע חִבְּק֖וּ אַשְׁפַּתֹּֽות׃ ס

[6] וַיִּגְדַּל֙ עֲוֹ֣ן בַּת־עַמִּ֔י מֵֽחַטַּ֖את סְדֹ֑ם הַֽהֲפוּכָ֣ה כְמֹו־רָ֔גַע וְלֹא־חָ֥לוּ בָ֖הּ יָדָֽיִם׃ ס

[7] זַכּ֤וּ נְזִירֶ֙יהָ֙ מִשֶּׁ֔לֶג צַח֖וּ מֵחָלָ֑ב אָ֤דְמוּ עֶ֙צֶם֙ מִפְּנִינִ֔ים סַפִּ֖יר גִּזְרָתָֽם׃ ס

[8] חָשַׁ֤ךְ מִשְּׁחֹור֙ תָּֽאֳרָ֔ם לֹ֥א נִכְּר֖וּ בַּחוּצֹ֑ות צָפַ֤ד עֹורָם֙ עַל־עַצְמָ֔ם יָבֵ֖שׁ הָיָ֥ה כָעֵֽץ׃ ס

[9] טֹובִ֤ים הָיוּ֙ חַלְלֵי־חֶ֔רֶב מֵֽחַלְלֵ֖י רָעָ֑ב שֶׁ֣הֵ֤ם יָז֙וּבוּ֙ מְדֻקָּרִ֔ים מִתְּנוּבֹ֖ת שָׂדָֽי׃ ס

[10] יְדֵ֗י נָשִׁים֙ רַחֲמָ֣נִיֹּ֔ות בִּשְּׁל֖וּ יַלְדֵיהֶ֑ן הָי֤וּ לְבָרֹות֙ לָ֔מֹו בְּשֶׁ֖בֶר בַּת־עַמִּֽי׃ ס

[11] כִּלָּ֤ה יְהוָה֙ אֶת־חֲמָתֹ֔ו שָׁפַ֖ךְ חֲרֹ֣ון אַפֹּ֑ו וַיַּצֶּת־אֵ֣שׁ בְּצִיֹּ֔ון וַתֹּ֖אכַל יְסֹודֹתֶֽיהָ׃ ס

pine away, being stricken For lack of the fruits of the field.

10 The hands of compassionate women Boiled their own children; They became food for them Because of the destruction of the daughter of my people.

11 The LORD has accomplished His wrath, He has poured out His fierce anger; And He has kindled a fire in Zion Which has consumed its foundations.

12 The kings of the earth did not believe, Nor *did* any of the inhabitants of the world, That the adversary and the enemy Could enter the gates of Jerusalem.

13 Because of the sins of her prophets *And* the iniquities of her priests, Who have shed in her midst The blood of the righteous;

14 They wandered, blind, in the streets; They were defiled with blood So that no one could touch their garments.

15 "Depart! Unclean!" they cried of themselves. "Depart, depart, do not touch!" So they fled and wandered; *Men* among the nations said, "They shall not continue to dwell *with us*."

16 The presence of the LORD has scattered them, He will not continue to regard them; They did not honor the priests, They did not favor the elders.

17 Yet our eyes failed, *Looking* for help was useless; In our watching we have watched For a nation that could not save.

18 They hunted our steps So that we could not walk in our streets; Our end drew near, Our days were finished For our end had come.

19 Our pursuers were swifter Than the eagles of the sky; They chased us on the mountains, They waited in ambush for us in the wilderness.

12 לֹא הֶאֱמִ֙ינוּ֙ מַלְכֵי־אֶ֔רֶץ (וְכל) [כֹּל] יֹשְׁבֵ֖י תֵבֵ֑ל כִּ֤י יָבֹא֙ צַ֣ר וְאוֹיֵ֔ב בְּשַׁעֲרֵ֖י יְרוּשָׁלָֽם׃ ס

13 מֵחַטֹּ֣את נְבִיאֶ֔יהָ עֲוֺנ֖וֹת כֹּהֲנֶ֑יהָ הַשֹּׁפְכִ֥ים בְּקִרְבָּ֖הּ דַּ֥ם צַדִּיקִֽים׃ ס

14 נָע֤וּ עִוְרִים֙ בַּֽחוּצ֔וֹת נְגֹֽאֲל֖וּ בַּדָּ֑ם בְּלֹ֣א יֽוּכְל֔וּ יִגְּע֖וּ בִּלְבֻשֵׁיהֶֽם׃ ס

15 ס֣וּרוּ טָמֵ֞א קָ֣רְאוּ לָ֗מוֹ ס֤וּרוּ ס֙וּרוּ֙ אַל־תִּגָּ֔עוּ כִּ֥י נָצ֖וּ גַּם־נָ֑עוּ אָֽמְרוּ֙ בַּגּוֹיִ֔ם לֹ֥א יוֹסִ֖פוּ לָגֽוּר׃ ס

16 פְּנֵ֤י יְהֹוָה֙ חִלְּקָ֔ם לֹ֥א יוֹסִ֖יף לְהַבִּיטָ֑ם פְּנֵ֤י כֹהֲנִים֙ לֹ֣א נָשָׂ֔אוּ (זקנים) [וּזְקֵנִ֖ים] לֹ֥א חָנָֽנוּ׃ ס

17 (עודינה) [עוֹדֵ֙ינוּ֙] תִּכְלֶ֣ינָה עֵינֵ֔ינוּ אֶל־עֶזְרָתֵ֖נוּ הָ֑בֶל בְּצִפִּיָּתֵ֣נוּ צִפִּ֔ינוּ אֶל־גּ֖וֹי לֹ֥א יוֹשִֽׁעַ׃ ס

18 צָד֣וּ צְעָדֵ֔ינוּ מִלֶּ֖כֶת בִּרְחֹבֹתֵ֑ינוּ קָרַ֥ב קִצֵּ֛ינוּ מָלְא֥וּ יָמֵ֖ינוּ כִּי־בָ֥א קִצֵּֽינוּ׃ ס

19 קַלִּ֤ים הָיוּ֙ רֹדְפֵ֔ינוּ מִנִּשְׁרֵ֖י שָׁמָ֑יִם עַל־הֶהָרִ֣ים דְּלָקֻ֔נוּ בַּמִּדְבָּ֖ר אָ֥רְבוּ לָֽנוּ׃ ס

20 ר֤וּחַ אַפֵּ֙ינוּ֙ מְשִׁ֣יחַ יְהֹוָ֔ה נִלְכַּ֖ד בִּשְׁחִיתוֹתָ֑ם אֲשֶׁ֣ר אָמַ֔רְנוּ בְּצִלּ֖וֹ נִֽחְיֶ֥ה בַגּוֹיִֽם׃ ס

21 שִׂ֤ישִׂי וְשִׂמְחִי֙ בַּת־אֱד֔וֹם (יושבתי) [יוֹשֶׁ֖בֶת] בְּאֶ֣רֶץ ע֑וּץ גַּם־עָלַ֙יִךְ֙ תַּעֲבָר־כּ֔וֹס תִּשְׁכְּרִ֖י וְתִתְעָרִֽי׃ ס

22 תַּם־עֲוֺנֵךְ֙ בַּת־צִיּ֔וֹן לֹ֥א יוֹסִ֖יף לְהַגְלוֹתֵ֑ךְ פָּקַ֤ד עֲוֺנֵךְ֙ בַּת־אֱד֔וֹם גִּלָּ֖ה עַל־חַטֹּאתָֽיִךְ׃ פ

[20] The breath of our nostrils, the LORD'S anointed, Was captured in their pits, Of whom we had said, "Under his shadow We shall live among the nations."

[21] Rejoice and be glad, O daughter of Edom, Who dwells in the land of Uz; *But* the cup will come around to you as well, You will become drunk and make yourself naked.

[22] *The punishment* of your iniquity has been completed, O daughter of Zion; He will exile you no longer. *But* He will punish your iniquity, O daughter of Edom; He will expose your sins!

Process of Discovery

Linguistics Section

Linguistic Structure

A[1] How dark the gold has become, *How* the pure gold has changed! The sacred stones are poured out At the corner of every street.

B [2] The precious sons of Zion, Weighed against fine gold, How they are regarded as earthen jars, The work of a potter's hands!

C [3] Even jackals offer the breast, They nurse their young; *But* the daughter of my people has become cruel Like ostriches in the wilderness.

D [4] The tongue of the infant cleaves To the roof of its mouth because of thirst; The little ones ask for bread, *But* no one breaks *it* for them.

E [5] Those who ate delicacies Are desolate in the streets; Those reared in purple Embrace ash pits.

F [6] For the iniquity of the daughter of my people Is greater than the sin of Sodom, Which was overthrown as in a moment, And no hands were turned toward her.

G [7] Her consecrated ones were purer than snow, They were whiter than milk; They were more ruddy *in* body than corals, Their polishing *was like* lapis lazuli.

H [8] Their appearance is blacker than soot, They are not recognized in the streets; Their skin is shriveled on their bones, It is withered, it has become like wood.

I [9] Better are those slain with the sword Than those slain with hunger; For they pine away, being stricken For lack of the fruits of the field.

J [10] The hands of compassionate women Boiled their own children; They became food for them Because of the destruction of the daughter of my people.

K [11] The LORD has accomplished His wrath, He has poured out His fierce anger; And He has kindled a fire in Zion Which has consumed its foundations.

K' [12] The kings of the earth did not believe, Nor *did* any of the inhabitants of the world, That the adversary and the enemy Could enter the gates of Jerusalem.

J'[13] Because of the sins of her prophets *And* the iniquities of her priests, Who have shed in her midst The blood of the righteous;

I' [14] They wandered, blind, in the streets; They were defiled with blood So that no one could touch their garments.

H' [15] "Depart! Unclean!" they cried of themselves. "Depart, depart, do not touch!" So they fled and wandered; *Men* among the nations said, "They shall not continue to dwell *with us*."

G' [16] The presence of the LORD has scattered them, He will not continue to regard them; They did not honor the priests, They did not favor the elders.

F' [17] Yet our eyes failed, *Looking* for help was useless; In our watching we have watched For a nation that could not save.

E' [18] They hunted our steps So that we could not walk in our streets; Our end drew near, Our days were finished For our end had come.

D' [19] Our pursuers were swifter Than the eagles of the sky; They chased us on the mountains, They waited in ambush for us in the wilderness.

C' [20] The breath of our nostrils, the LORD'S anointed, Was captured in their pits, Of whom we had said, "Under his shadow We shall live among the nations."

B' [21] Rejoice and be glad, O daughter of Edom, Who dwells in the land of Uz; *But* the cup will come around to you as well, You will become drunk and make yourself naked.

A' [22] *The punishment* of your iniquity has been completed, O daughter of Zion; He will exile you no longer. *But* He will punish your iniquity, O daughter of Edom; He will expose your sins!

A: Captivity. B: Vessel. C: To rely on. D: Sufferings. E: Town. F: Foreign country. G: Priests. H: Dirty. I: Bloody. J: Sacrifice. K: Destruction of Jerusalem.[47]

Discussion

This chapter is another deep chiasm.

Questioning the Passage

1. What is the meaning of verse one?

    The gold symbolizes the people of Jerusalem.[48] The gold became dull because the conquered people of Jerusalem were sad about the destruction of the city and Temple. Their faces would show their despair. The sacred stones are the children who were killed in the streets.

2. What is the meaning of verse two?

    The sons of Jerusalem were valuable to the nation, but they were killed or captured. They were destroyed like the pottery of the city.

3. What is the meaning of verse three?

    The Sage Rashi said that this verse meant that the mothers of Jerusalem became cruel to their children because of the famine. Jewish mothers always took care of

---

[47] Hajime Murai, "Literary Structure (Chiasm, Chiasmus) of Book of Lamentations," Literary structure (chiasm, chiasmus) of each pericopes of Book of Lamentations, accessed April 21, 2020, http://www.bible.literarystructure.info/bible/25_Lamentations_pericope_e.html.

[48] Zlotowitz, Meir, and Nosson Scherman. "Chapter 4." *Megillas Eichah = Lamentations: A New Translation with a Commentary Anthologized from Talmudic, Midrashic and Rabbinic Sources*. New York: Mesorah Publications, 1979. N. pag. Print.

their children first. However, they allowed their children to go hungry during the starvation and siege. They ignored their children's cries for help.[49]

4. What does verse four mean?

   This verse is connected to verse three. The mothers who let their babies starve would not breastfeed them. If they had done so, they would have died sooner.

5. What does "no hands were turned towards her" mean? (v. 6)

   The LORD destroyed the city of Sodom by sending fireballs from Heaven upon the city. The city of Jerusalem suffered a similar fate, except that the fireballs were not from Heaven but rather from the Babylonian army

6. Who are the consecrated ones in verse seven?

   The Targum indicates that the consecrated ones were Nazirites of the city. Verse eight describes what the Nazirites of the town looked like after the destruction of the city. [50]

7. What does verse twelve mean?

   The attack by Sennacherib, ruler of the Assyrians, could not defeat the city of Jerusalem. The world's nations were shocked when they learned that Nebuchadnezzar did what Sennacherib could not do.[51]

---

[49] IBID.

[50] Martin McNamara, Kevin J. Cathcart, and Michael Maher, *The Aramaic Bible: the Targums* (Wilmington, DE: M. Glazier, 1987).

[51] Zlotowitz, Meir, and Nosson Scherman. "Chapter 4." *Megillas Eichah = Lamentations: A New Translation with a Commentary Anthologized from Talmudic, Midrashic and Rabbinic Sources.* New York: Mesorah Publications, 1979. N. pag. Print.

8. What were the sins of her prophets in verse thirteen?

The Targum reads "false prophets."[52] There were several false prophets in Judea during the Babylonian invasion. Jeremiah says that the false prophets led the leaders astray from proper worship of the LORD.

9. What does "unclean" mean? (v. 15)

When blood has been shed or touched, the individual becomes unclean. If the unclean person felt another person, that person was unclean. Many people were lying in the streets, bleeding to death. Many people walked around the city while bleeding. The people unaffected did not want to be touched by a bleeding person.

10. What is verse eighteen to twenty describing?

These verses described what life was like for the few people who remained in Jerusalem after the attack was over.[53] Living under Babylonian rule in a destroyed city was not easy. It also tells us that not all the residents of Jerusalem were removed. About fifteen percent of the population was taken to Babylon. The rest were left to fend for themselves.

11. What does verse twenty-one mean?

The Edomites lived south of Judea. As people fled Judea, if they traveled into Edom, they stood a chance of being caught. Jews who were caught were sold to the Babylonians. Jeremiah said that the punishment upon Jerusalem was brought

---

[52] Martin McNamara, Kevin J. Cathcart, and Michael Maher, *The Aramaic Bible: the Targums* (Wilmington, DE: M. Glazier, 1987).

[53] Zlotowitz, Meir, and Nosson Scherman. "Chapter 4." *Megillas Eichah = Lamentations: A New Translation with a Commentary Anthologized from Talmudic, Midrashic and Rabbinic Sources*. New York: Mesorah Publications, 1979. N. pag. Print.

on by the LORD and was complete with the city's destruction. Edom would be punished at some future time because they assisted in Jerusalem's destruction.

Thoughts

This is another chapter of Jeremiah's lament about the destruction of the city of Jerusalem. Jeremiah found additional allegorical ways to talk about the famine, the siege, and the destruction of Jerusalem. The people of Jerusalem brought this on by their disobedience. The people entered into a contract with the LORD at Mount Sinai. They offered to follow the ways of the LORD, and the LORD offered His protection. The people, especially the leaders, broke that covenant. The LORD took away His protection, which allowed the powerful Babylonian army to invade. By doing so, Nebuchadnezzar could stretch his trade routes practically to Egypt. If he had captured a bit more, he could have sent troops to conquer Egypt.

Michael Harvey Koplitz

Chapter Five

Language

New American Standard 1995	Hebrew
[1] Remember, O LORD, what has befallen us; Look, and see our reproach! [2] Our inheritance has been turned over to strangers, Our houses to aliens. [3] We have become orphans without a father, Our mothers are like widows. [4] We have to pay for our drinking water, Our wood comes *to us* at a price. [5] Our pursuers are at our necks; We are worn out, there is no rest for us. [6] We have submitted to Egypt *and* Assyria to get enough bread. [7] Our fathers sinned, *and* are no more; It is we who have borne their iniquities. [8] Slaves rule over us; There is no one to deliver us from their hand. [9] We get our bread at the risk of our lives Because of the sword in the wilderness. [10] Our skin has become as hot as an oven, Because of the burning heat of famine. [11] They ravished the women in Zion, The virgins in the cities of Judah. [12] Princes were hung by their hands; Elders were not respected. [13] Young men worked at the grinding mill, And youths stumbled under *loads* of wood. [14] Elders are gone from the gate, Young men from their music. [15] The joy of our hearts has ceased; Our dancing has been turned into mourning. [16] The crown has fallen from our head; Woe to us, for we have sinned!	זְכֹר יְהוָה מֶה־הָיָה לָנוּ (הַבֵּיט) [הַבִּיטָה] וּרְאֵה אֶת־חֶרְפָּתֵנוּ: 2 נַחֲלָתֵנוּ נֶהֶפְכָה לְזָרִים בָּתֵּינוּ לְנָכְרִים: 3 יְתוֹמִים הָיִינוּ (אֵין) [וְאֵין] אָב אִמֹּתֵינוּ כְּאַלְמָנוֹת: 4 מֵימֵינוּ בְּכֶסֶף שָׁתִינוּ עֵצֵינוּ בִּמְחִיר יָבֹאוּ: 5 עַל צַוָּארֵנוּ נִרְדָּפְנוּ יָגַעְנוּ (לֹא) [וְלֹא] הוּנַח לָנוּ: 6 מִצְרַיִם נָתַנּוּ יָד אַשּׁוּר לִשְׂבֹּעַ לָחֶם: 7 אֲבֹתֵינוּ חָטְאוּ (אֵינָם) [וְאֵינָם] (אֲנַחְנוּ) [וַאֲנַחְנוּ] עֲוֹנֹתֵיהֶם סָבָלְנוּ: 8 עֲבָדִים מָשְׁלוּ בָנוּ פֹּרֵק אֵין מִיָּדָם: 9 בְּנַפְשֵׁנוּ נָבִיא לַחְמֵנוּ מִפְּנֵי חֶרֶב הַמִּדְבָּר: 10 עוֹרֵנוּ כְּתַנּוּר נִכְמָרוּ מִפְּנֵי זַלְעֲפוֹת רָעָב: 11 נָשִׁים בְּצִיּוֹן עִנּוּ בְּתֻלֹת בְּעָרֵי יְהוּדָה: 12 שָׂרִים בְּיָדָם נִתְלוּ פְּנֵי זְקֵנִים לֹא נֶהְדָּרוּ: 13 בַּחוּרִים טְחוֹן נָשָׂאוּ וּנְעָרִים בָּעֵץ כָּשָׁלוּ: 14 זְקֵנִים מִשַּׁעַר שָׁבָתוּ בַּחוּרִים מִנְּגִינָתָם: 15 שָׁבַת מְשׂוֹשׂ לִבֵּנוּ נֶהְפַּךְ לְאֵבֶל מְחֹלֵנוּ: 16 נָפְלָה עֲטֶרֶת רֹאשֵׁנוּ אוֹי־נָא לָנוּ כִּי חָטָאנוּ: 17 עַל־זֶה הָיָה דָוֶה לִבֵּנוּ עַל־אֵלֶּה חָשְׁכוּ עֵינֵינוּ: 18 עַל הַר־צִיּוֹן שֶׁשָּׁמֵם שׁוּעָלִים הִלְּכוּ־בוֹ: פ 19 אַתָּה יְהוָה לְעוֹלָם תֵּשֵׁב כִּסְאֲךָ לְדֹר וָדוֹר: 20 לָמָּה לָנֶצַח תִּשְׁכָּחֵנוּ תַּעַזְבֵנוּ לְאֹרֶךְ יָמִים: 21 הֲשִׁיבֵנוּ יְהוָה אֵלֶיךָ (וְנָשׁוּב) [וְנָשׁוּבָה] חַדֵּשׁ יָמֵינוּ כְּקֶדֶם: 22 כִּי אִם־מָאֹס מְאַסְתָּנוּ קָצַפְתָּ עָלֵינוּ עַד־מְאֹד:

<table>
<tr><td>

¹⁷ Because of this our heart is faint, Because of these things our eyes are dim;
¹⁸ Because of Mount Zion which lies desolate, Foxes prowl in it.
¹⁹ You, O LORD, rule forever; Your throne is from generation to generation.
²⁰ Why do You forget us forever? Why do You forsake us so long?
²¹ Restore us to You, O LORD, that we may be restored; Renew our days as of old,
²² Unless You have utterly rejected us *And* are exceedingly angry with us.

</td><td></td></tr>
</table>

Process of Discovery

Linguistics Section

Linguistic Structure

A ¹ Remember, O LORD, what has befallen us; Look, and see our reproach! ² Our inheritance has been turned over to strangers, Our houses to aliens. ³ We have become orphans without a father, Our mothers are like widows. ⁴ We have to pay for our drinking water, Our wood comes *to us* at a price. ⁵ Our pursuers are at our necks; We are worn out, there is no rest for us.

    B ⁶ We have submitted to Egypt *and* Assyria to get enough bread. ⁷ Our fathers sinned, *and* are no more; It is we who have borne their iniquities. ⁸ Slaves rule over us; There is no one to deliver us from their hand. ⁹ We get our bread at the risk of our lives Because of the sword in the wilderness.

        C ¹⁰ Our skin has become as hot as an oven, Because of the burning heat of famine. ¹¹ They ravished the women in Zion, The virgins in the cities of Judah. ¹² Princes were hung by their hands; Elders were not respected. ¹³ Young men worked at the grinding mill, And youths stumbled under *loads* of wood. ¹⁴ Elders are gone from the gate, Young men from their music. ¹⁵ The joy of our hearts has ceased; Our dancing has been turned into mourning.

    B' ¹⁶ The crown has fallen from our head; Woe to us, for we have sinned! ¹⁷ Because of this our heart is faint, Because of these things our eyes are dim; ¹⁸ Because of Mount Zion which lies desolate, Foxes prowl in it.

A' ¹⁹ You, O LORD, rule forever; Your throne is from generation to generation. ²⁰ Why do You forget us forever? Why do You forsake us so long? ²¹ Restore us to You, O LORD, that we may be restored; Renew our days as of old, ²² Unless You have utterly rejected us *And* are exceedingly angry with us.

    A: To be forsaken. B: Sins. C: Lamentation.[54]

---

[54] Hajime Murai, "Literary Structure (Chiasm, Chiasmus) of Book of Lamentations," Literary structure (chiasm, chiasmus) of each pericopes of Book of Lamentations, accessed April 21, 2020, http://www.bible.literarystructure.info/bible/25_Lamentations_pericope_e.html.

Discussion

This chapter of Lamentations describes Jerusalem at the end of the Babylonian siege and the destruction of the city and the Temple.

Questioning the Passage

1. Who are the slaves mentioned in verse eight?

   The Targum says that the slaves are the sons of Ham (one of Noah's sons). The sons of Shem (another son of Noah) were to rule over Ham. The opposite had occurred. The sons of Ham are the Egyptians.[55]

   Another interpretation is that the slaves are the people of Edom. Before the Babylonian invasion, Edom was paying tribute to Judah. After the invasion, Edom captured Jews escaping captivity. Edom sold these Jews to the Babylonians.[56]

2. What is verse thirteen referring to?

   The Sage Rashi said that the Babylonians forced the young men to carry millstones on their shoulders to drain them of their strength.[57]

---

[55] Martin McNamara, Kevin J. Cathcart, and Michael Maher, *The Aramaic Bible: the Targums* (Wilmington, DE: M. Glazier, 1987).

[56] Zlotowitz, Meir, and Nosson Scherman. "Chapter 4." *Megillas Eichah = Lamentations: A New Translation with a Commentary Anthologized from Talmudic, Midrashic and Rabbinic Sources.* New York: Mesorah Publications, 1979. N. pag. Print.

[57] IBID.

Phrase Study

1. כָּמַר (kāmar) "I, yearn, be kindled, be black (ASV similar, RSV instead of "be black" has "be hot.")

   The root meaning is to be warm, and hot. Three of the four occurrences (Gen 43:30; 1 Kgs 3:26; Hos 11:8) are Niphal expressing the emotions of filial attachments, in the latter case, those of God for his people."[58]

Culture Section

Questioning the passage

1. Why is it noted that water and food had to be purchased? (v. 5)

   Before the invasion, villages, and towns had a water supply available to the people. Water was not paid for; instead, water was retrieved from the stream or well of the village. Wood for burning was gathered and was free. In a city like Jerusalem, water and wood cost money. After the invasion, the people in the villages had to pay for water and wood because everything became scarce. After all, the Babylonian army took whatever it needed leaving the people very little.[59]

2. What does "we have submitted" mean in verse five?

   This Aramaic idiom means, "we have surrendered to our enemies." Judea expected its allies, the remaining Assyrians and Egypt, to come to their rescue. Judea's allies disappeared when the Babylonians invaded.[60]

---

[58]Robert Laird. Harris, *Theological Word Book of the Old Testament*, 1981.
[59] Lamsa, George M., Rocco Errico A. "Lamentations Chapter 1." In *Aramaic Light on Isaiah, Jeremiah, and Lamentations*, by Smyrna: Noorah, 2011
[60] IBID

3. What does "our skin was black like an oven" mean in verse ten?

   "Black" is a better and more accurate translation than "hot," which is used in the New American Standard. Black is considered an unlucky color among Semitic people. Black symbolizes death, mourning, suffering, distress, and difficulties. When Near Eastern people suffered from famine or persecution, they would say that "our skin is black." The siege of Jerusalem caused famine and the persecution of the people.[61]

Thoughts

This final chapter of the book of Lamentations recaps the sin and the invasion of the Babylonian army. The last three verses bring a light of hope. Jeremiah calls out to the LORD to restore the people and the nation. He confesses the sins of the people to the LORD. He asks for forgiveness for what the past brought.

---

[61] IBID.

Bibliography

Davis, Anne Kimball. 2012. *The Synoptic Gospels.*

Laird, Robert. 1981. *Theological Word Book of the Old Testament.*

Lamsa, George, Rocco Errico. 2011. *Lamentations in Aramaic Light on Isaiah, Jeremiah, and Lamentations.* Smyrna, GA: Noorah Foundation.

Lamsa, Rocco A. Errico and George M. 2010. *Aramaic Light on Ezra through the Song of Solomon.* Smyma, GA: Noohra Foundation.

Martin McNamara, Kevin J. Cathcart, and Michael Maher. 1987. *The Aramaic Bible: The Targums.* Wilminton, DE: M. Glazier.

Murai, Hajime. n.d. *Literary Structure (Chiasm, Chiasmus) of the Book of Lamentations.* Accessed April 21, 2020. http://www.bible.literarystructure.info/bible/25_Lamentations_pericope_e.html.

1986. *Back to School.* Directed by Paper Clip Productions.

n.d. *The Seven Annual Sacred Feasts of the Old Cove.* Accessed May 1, 2020. http://www.agapebiblestudy.com/charts/Seven%20Sacred%20Feasts%20of%20the%20Old%20Covenant.htm.

2016. *Tributary.* September 28. Accessed April 28, 2020. http://wikipedia.com.

Zlotowitz, Meir and Nossom Scherman. 1979. *Megillas Eichach - Lamentations.* New York: New York: Mesorah Publications.

[i] Rabbi Solomon ben Isaac (Shlomo Yitzhaki), known as Rashi (based on an acronym of his Hebrew initials), is one of the most influential Jewish commentators in history. He was born in Troyes, Champagne, in northern France, in 1040.

At age 17, Rashi received an education in the yeshiva of Rabbi Yaakov ben Yakar in Worms, where the "Rashi Chapel" was built years after his death (this chapel was subsequently destroyed during the German occupation in World War II, and rebuilt in 1950). At age 25, he returned to Troyes, where he became a rabbi. Since rabbis were not yet paid officials at this point in time, Rashi also worked with his family in the local vineyards. In 1070, he founded a yeshiva where he taught many disciples, some of whom would also go on to become prominent Jewish scholars. In 1096, Rashi witnessed the massacre of friends and family members at the hands of Crusaders en route to the Holy Land. He died in 1105 in Troyes. Source: https://www.myjewishlearning.com/article/who-was-rashi/

[ii] Renowned as one of the great *darshanim* (sermonizers) of the Jewish world, Rabbi Moshe Alshich was born in Adrianople, Turkey in 5268 (1508 CE) but lived most of his long and productive life in Safed. In his youth, he studied in the yeshivas headed by Rabbi Yosef Caro in Adrianople and Rabbi Yosef Taitatzak in Salonica. Rabbi Moshe revered Rabbi Yosef Caro and referred to him on occasion as "my father." At a relatively young age, he left for Israel together with Rabbi Caro and settled in Safed. There he was ordained by Rabbi Yosef Caro, eventually serving as one of the judges in Rabbi Yosef Caro's rabbinical court. The story is told that one day it was revealed to Rabbi Caro that his student had merited one of the seventy facets of Torah exegesis. Accordingly, Rabbi Caro compelled Rabbi Moshe to deliver the sermon on that Sabbath. The sermon was received with great acclaim, and from then on, Rabbi Moshe was given the unsought for honor of delivering a sermon every week. From

these sermons, his famous *"Torat Moshe"* on the Pentateuch was compiled. Source: https://www.chabad.org/kabbalah/article_cdo/aid/380688/jewish/Rabbi-Moshe-Alshich.htm

[iii] In 1492, the Jews were expelled from Spain. Some went West to discover the Americas, yet the bulk went East to Turkey, and it was in the beginning of the sixteenth century that a number of Jews settled in the Holy Land in the city of Safed.

For an eighty year period there was a renaissance of Jewish life and activity in this mystical city that was to change and shape the Jewish world.

The rabbi of the city was none other than the famous Rabbi Joseph Karo. After writing his monumental work called the Bet Yosef, in which he traces the source and origin of contemporary Jewish Law, he summarized all practical legalistics in his book the Code of Jewish Law (*Shulchan Aruch*).

The city's mystics were no less famous. Rabbi Moses Cordevero, known as the Ramak, wrote a monumental Kabbalistic work called Pardes Rimonim. However, the most famous Kabbalist of the day was Rabbi Isaac Luria (1534-1572), universally known as the Arizal, an acronym for "The G-dly Rabbi Isaac of Blessed Memory."

Though the Arizal only lived for 38 years, he possessed a phenomenal soul, and all secrets of the creation were open to him. It was only in the last two years of his life that he met his foremost disciple, Rabbi Chaim Vital. While the Arizal himself never wrote any books, however all his words were faithfully recorded by Rabbi Chaim Vittal and recorded in what we call Kitvei Ari, the "writings of the Arizal." Source: https://www.chabad.org/library/article_cdo/aid/361878/jewish/The-Arizal.htm

[iv] Samuel de Uçeda שמואל די אוזידא (1604 - 1545 CE) (לספירה 1604 - 1545)
"16th century Rosh Yeshiva and Kabbalist in Safed, disciple of the Arizal and R' Hayyim Vital. He established a large Yeshiva in Safed which promoted the study of Halacha and

Kabbalah. His most famous work is "Midrash Shmuel" on Pirkei Avot, which contains an anthology of other commentaries along with his own insights. He also wrote commentaries on the Megillot: "Iggeret Shmuel" on Ruth, and "Lechem Dimah" on Eichah. His commentary on Esther has been recently published." Source: https://www.sefaria.org/person/Samuel%20de%20Uceda